Praise for *A*

What is so astonish
their ceaseless and steadfast readiness to stand up for their principles
at any price. Yet despite this, they are also the most open individuals, with a great capacity for engagement with others. They are much
more than friends.
— Ayed Morrar, founder of Palestinian Popular Resistance
Committees

Anarchists Against the Wall is one of the most courageous,
committed groups working against the occupation. They go where
other Israelis are afraid to go, place themselves regularly in physical
and emotional danger, and build a whole new level of alliances with
Palestinians working nonviolently for justice. This collection of their
writings and reflections is a vital contribution to our understanding
of the situation, and should be read by everyone who is concerned
with justice and peace in the Middle East. It shows a dimension of
the struggle that the media mostly ignore, and will broaden your
sense of the possibilities for unlikely alliances and coalitions across
boundaries.
— Starhawk, author of *The Empowerment Manual*

The only thing stopping the state of Israel from declaring these
anti-Zionists as non-Israelis is that it will be contradicting its own
rhetoric. The state will be pulling the trigger that will blow away its
rhetoric that "Israel is the home of all the Jews." This will be the start
of the end.
— Ma'ath Musleh, Palestinian journalist and activist

ANARCHISTS
AGAINST THE WALL

DIRECT ACTION AND SOLIDARITY WITH THE PALESTINIAN POPULAR STRUGGLE

Anarchists Against the Wall: Direct Action and Solidarity with the Palestinian Popular Struggle edited by Uri Gordon and Ohal Grietzer

ISBN: 978-1-84935-114-0 | Ebook: 978-1-84935-115-7
Library of Congress Number: 2012914343

Cover Design and Interior: Josh MacPhee/Antumbradesign.org
Illustrations: Josh MacPhee (the illustration on 42 is based on a photograph by Activestills.org)

Printed in the USA on recycled, acid-free paper.

AK Press, 674-A 23rd Street, Oakland, CA 94612
www.akpress.org | akpress@akpress.org | 510.208.1700

AK Press UK, P.O. Box 12766, Edinburgh EH8 9YE
www.akuk.com | ak@akedin.demon.co.uk | 0131.555.5165

Institute for Anarchist Studies, P.O. Box 15586, Washington, DC 20003
www.anarchist-studies.org | info@anarchiststudies.org

At least 50 percent of the net sales from each title in the Anarchist Interventions series are donated to the IAS, thanks to the generosity of each author. All other proceeds from this title will be donated to the Anarchists Against the Wall legal defense fund.

ANARCHISTS AGAINST THE WALL

DIRECT ACTION AND SOLIDARITY WITH THE PALESTINIAN POPULAR STRUGGLE

Edited by Uri Gordon and Ohal Grietzer

Foreword by Alfredo M. Bonanno

AK Press / Institute for Anarchist Studies | 2013

Anarchist Interventions:
An IAS/AK Press Book Series

Radical ideas can open up spaces for radical actions, by illuminating hierarchical power relations and drawing out possibilities for liberatory social transformations. The Anarchist Interventions series—a collaborative project between the Institute for Anarchist Studies (IAS) and AK Press—strives to contribute to the development of relevant, vital anarchist theory and analysis by intervening in contemporary discussions. Works in this series look at twenty-first-century social conditions—including social structures and oppression, their historical trajectories, and new forms of domination, to name a few—as well as reveal opportunities for different tomorrows premised on horizontal, egalitarian forms of self-organization.

Given that anarchism has become the dominant tendency within revolutionary milieus and movements today, it is crucial that anarchists explore current phenomena, strategies, and visions in a much more rigorous, serious manner. Each title in this series, then, features present-day anarchist voices, with the aim, over time, of publishing a variety of perspectives. The series' multifaceted goals are to cultivate anarchist thought so as to better inform anarchist practice, encourage a culture of public intellectuals and constructive debate within anarchism, introduce new generations to anarchism, and offer insights into today's world and potentialities for a freer society.

Contents

Foreword

The wall is there, where before it was not. It is a horrible, gigantic artifact that continues for hundreds of kilometers, adapting itself, overstepping the more or less internationally accepted "borders," growing in height, or transforming itself into trenches or other structures designed to isolate the "enemy."

I know some of the places where it rises—for example, Tulkarem, Qalqiliya, and Gush Etzion south of Jerusalem—very well.

But that is not the point. A wall is built of stones and cement. A trench is a hole dug many meters into the ground, assisted by barbed wire, an electronic mechanism, a revolving door. All mute objects desired by fear and imposed by force. These things are not the fundamental point of a *human distance* that has been dug between Israelis and Palestinians for so long, to the point of becoming *almost* insurmountable.

At the origin of this distance there is the fear of those who, in a past so remote that by now it seems archaic, could have worked with the "first wave" of settlers, yet gradually became, if not exactly their armed enemy, cheap labor to be utilized. And then, slowly, in the unfolding of decades of political and international errors or swindles, and the shirking of all kinds of leaders (and parties and sides), that fear has turned into a solid object that is far higher and harder than any wall could ever be.

How can you get close to someone made vicious through rejection and confinement, to someone who wallows in the mud of refugee camps, to someone who feeds on the crazy ideology of "throw them all into the sea," to someone who shoots his Qassams built in the courtyard into the sky thick with clouds? And on the other hand, how can you approach those who see the wall and all its hideous aspects as the only defense against an enemy who has always been painted aggressively as someone forever ill-disposed to any agreement? What to say about certain demonstrations in defense of segregation?

In my opinion, one should not reduce the problem to a mere propaganda issue. It is not just a question of *denouncing* the abuse committed with the construction of more than seven hundred kilometers of wall, or the shame of this ghettoization, which Jews more than anyone in the world should consider horrible and unacceptable. We must go a step further.

One should not limit oneself to working with Palestinians, to seeing them as brothers and not as enemies to be softened by showing how not all Jews are in favour of this concrete monster that screams revenge to the skies. We must take another step further.

And what should this step be?

Attack. Demonstrative at first, for goodness sake! I do not want to talk about a definitive attack, as basically only the militarist illusion feeds off this kind of thing to the point of indigestion. I mean an attack on the concrete targets that establish, nurture, guarantee, justify, and finance the management of such a monstrosity as the wall in question.

It is not enough to simply call oneself "Anarchists Against the Wall" if the wall stays there in front of our noses as the emblem of the historical inevitability of the decisions of those in power, of those who have usurped the original libertarian expressions of the first Israeli settlements.

Huge actions? Thousands of people brought out into the streets? Fraternizing between Jews and Palestinians such as to make the windows of the Knesset quake? Yes, possibly that too, but also something else besides.

After all, anarchists, even on their own, have historically been capable of carrying out actions of attack, which in their small dimensions and reproducibility have inspired those who suffer exclusion, exploitation, and genocide.

And this last word, believe me, was not chosen at random.

The fact is that reality is right before our eyes. It does not need grand theories, or particular technical or strategic explanations. Just as that handful of women and men who became aware of its existence did not require any particular illumination. Often this fundamental condition of existence—the gaining awareness of a condition of tyranny that some are suffering, whether a few or many, individuals or entire peoples, is a problem that comes later—once set in motion cannot be stopped by anyone.

And who would be able to stop our action, our action as anarchists?

Do we need the charismatic signal of some leader perhaps? Some sort of strategic directorate made up of a handful of imbeciles declaring themselves a point of reference? Certainly not.

We have to attack. Everything else is just a form of support, essential but not of vital importance.

We know the crime that casts a shadow over our horizon by blocking the light of the sun. We know who the poor are, paying the consequences day in, day out. We know who is responsible, beyond the flags or religious choices that are more or less rooted in our forefathers' atavism.[1]

We need nothing else.

> —Alfredo M. Bonanno
> Trieste, February 26, 2012
> Translated by Jean Weir

Introduction

These are bleak times in the Eastern Mediterranean. Far from moving toward a just end, the Israeli occupation of the West Bank deepens daily. Jewish settlements continue to expand, while Palestinian homes, wells, and olive groves continue to be destroyed. Millions of Palestinians living under Israeli martial law continue to endure a decades-old system of oppression that denies them access to adequate medical services and education, obstructs them from traveling freely between their villages and cities, and surrounds their homes with a cement wall twenty-six feet high.

Palestinian refugees, expelled from their lands in 1948 and 1967, are still denied return or compensation, while Palestinian citizens of Israel are subjected to systematic discrimination. In Gaza, Israel has withdrawn its troops and settlers but has substituted a siege, restricting supplies and using mathematical formulas to keep the inhabitants alive on the verge of malnutrition.

Yet in all this darkness, one ray of hope continues to shine: a relentless Palestinian popular resistance movement, which embodies all that is dignified and human about the struggle for freedom and equality in this land. Marching, unarmed, toward confiscated lands and blocked roads. Defying tear gas, beatings and bullets, nightly raids, and trumped-up charges. Raising awareness and sustaining families. And all the while, extending an open hand to Israelis and internationals to join the struggle.

The struggle against the occupation is led by Palestinians, and Israeli (or international) solidarity on the ground should always be carried out in full recognition of the asymmetry created by our privilege. Yet for better or worse, the action initiative called Anarchists Against the Wall (AAtW) has become a source of inspiration well beyond the Middle East. And while it is likely that international comrades project more of their aspirations and hopes on us than we deserve, there is also legitimate space to relate the experiences and reflections of disobedient Israelis who oppose their own state's militaristic policies and rhetoric in the most unmediated way. And so we offer this book.

AAtW began its activity in late 2003, when a loose group of activists formed a direct action initiative to oppose the construction of Israel's so-called separation barrier. The group coalesced in the village of Mas'ha, where together with international and Palestinian activists, we all set up a protest camp on the planned route of the wall. A typical sentiment among activists in the group was the rejection of the old tactics of the Israeli peace movement—lobbying, electoral efforts, and interfaith dialogue—as ineffectual and paternalistic. Instead, they drew inspiration from the international anarchist and alter-globalization movements as well as the experiences of existing solidarity efforts that had formed since the eruption of the al-Aqsa Intifada—the second, armed Palestinian uprising in October 2000.

In fact, AAtW's inception can be traced back to the fusion of parallel undercurrents in Palestine and Israel during the second Intifada. In the West Bank and Gaza Strip, although significantly more militarized than the first, the second Intifada contained widespread instances of popular struggle and civilian resistance, such as direct actions, protests and demonstrations, nongovernmental organization initiatives, independent information and media efforts, youth projects, boycott campaigns, and civil disobedience, usually led by local popular committees. Marginalized as they were by the levels of violence and increasing hierarchical centralization of the Palestinian Authority, these efforts nevertheless managed to put down roots and eventually bear fruit. In Israel, the failure of the Oslo Accords resulted in a general nationalist entrenchment and shift to the right, including within the so-called Peace Camp. This had the opposite effect on those at the far Left end of the spectrum, however, as the realization of *why* Oslo failed led many to permanently let go of the coattails of the Zionist Left.

Initially, the major organ for Israeli solidarity with Palestinian communities was Ta'ayush ("living-together" in Arabic), a network that at its peak had hundreds of active participants, both Jews and Palestinian citizens of Israel. Ta'ayush activists brought food to besieged cities and towns, and defended Palestinian farmers from settlers and soldiers as they cultivated their land. In summer 2001, many international activists began arriving in Palestine as volunteers in the International Solidarity Movement

(ISM), a Palestinian-led coordination that accompanied nonviolent Palestinian actions in the West Bank. ISM actions included forming human chains to block soldiers from interfering while Palestinians tore down military roadblocks, held mass demonstrations, or collectively broke curfews to take children to school or tend their fields.

In spring 2002, with the intensification of Israeli violence in the West Bank, including the destruction of the Jenin refugee camp and siege of the Church of the Nativity in Bethlehem, the ISM was driven to more defensive activities including human shielding and live witnessing. ISM activists stayed in Palestinian homes facing demolition, rode with ambulances, escorted municipal workers to fix infrastructures, and delivered food and medicine to besieged communities. Israeli soldiers killed two ISM activists, Rachel Corrie and Tom Hurndall, in the Gaza Strip in 2003.

The protest camp in Mas'ha formed the opportunity for Israelis who had cooperated with ISM affinity groups to give more visibility to their own resistance as Israelis. The camp became a center of information and struggle against the planned construction of the barrier, which was just starting to be built at the time. Over its four-month duration, more than a thousand internationals and Israelis came to learn about the situation and join the struggle. Activists also cut the fence and destroyed parts of it. At one such action in December 2003, Israeli soldiers shot an Israeli activist named Gil Na'amati in both his legs with live ammunition from close range. The large amount of publicity that this incident received fixed the group's previously rotating name as the name picked for that action: Anarchists Against the Wall.

At this point, several Palestinian villages that were about to lose much of their lands to the wall formed popular committees to resist the construction. The connections made during the Mas'ha camp led to Israelis being invited to join those demonstrations, and the beginning of a long-term partnership between AAtW and popular committees in many villages. Demonstrations and actions took place almost daily in Budrus, Salem, Anin, Biddu, Beit Awwa, Deir Balut, Beit Surik, Beit Likia, and other villages as well as in Palestinian neighborhoods that were effectively imprisoned by the walls around Jerusalem. In a few actions, Palestinians and Israelis managed to halt construction work for the day, tear down or damage sections of the fence, or break through gates along it.

The pragmatic goal of the Israeli and international presence was to force the army to reduce its level of violent repression, since it has stricter rules of engagement when outsiders are present alongside Palestinians. Nevertheless, to date over twenty Palestinians have been killed in these demonstrations—sometimes by live ammunition, but more often by direct hits from allegedly less lethal weapons such as rubber-coated metal bullets and tear gas canisters.

Starting in February 2005, AAtW began to support weekly demonstrations in the village of Bil'in—to this day, a resilient mobilization sustained in numbers that has become an internationally recognized symbol of the popular struggle. In Bil'in as well as other villages, including Ni'ilin, Ma'asra, Beit Ummar, and Nabi Saleh, a regular pattern of Friday demonstrations was formed. A typical demonstration begins with a rally in the village center following Friday prayers, after which the residents and their supporters march toward the fence, or toward lands that have been taken over by settlers. Israeli soldiers sometimes will invade the village before the demonstration has started. At other times, the protesters will be able to reach the fence and chant slogans. In either case, the army inevitably declares the area a "closed military zone," and proceeds to disperse the demonstrators using tear gas, concussion grenades, rubber-coated metal bullets, shoving and beating. As the demonstration retreats back to the village, youths from the village frequently move to the rearguard and begin throwing stones at the Israeli forces, which sometimes invade the village for a number of hours. By sundown all is usually quiet again, though night raids are common.

Mass demonstrations are only one part of the Palestinian-led actions that Israelis and internationals join. Other endeavors include planting trees, rebuilding demolished homes and wells, and regularly accompanying Palestinian farmers or herders who face violence from Jewish settlers. The solidarity activists try to stand as a barrier between the attacking settlers and farmers, who sometimes manage to work their land for an hour or two. Israeli soldiers are usually present at these events, but stand by doing nothing, or else join the violent attacks and arrest farmers and activists. AAtW has also organized many antioccupation demonstrations and actions inside Israel. Activists have stretched barbed wire and set up a mock checkpoint in affluent north Tel Aviv, and briefly mounted Israeli tanks and armored personnel carriers preparing for an incursion into the Gaza Strip. In addition, there was widespread anarchist participation in the Israeli opposition to the August 2006 war on Lebanon and December 2008 war on Gaza. Anarchists formed large contingents in the demonstrations against these offensives and briefly blockaded the entrance to an air force base at the height of both wars. Other protests and direct actions inside Israel continue on an almost-weekly basis.

The pieces collected in this book are divided in two parts. The first contains short statements, including leaflets issued by AAtW in its early days or speeches given by its members on different occasions. The second part contains accounts, essays, and reflections by activists who participate in the group's actions. Some of these were written especially for this collection, and others were previously published in AAtW zines and other media. We hope they will provide readers with insights into the challenges presented by our struggle as well as the motivations and emotions of the participants.

While some of the pieces in the first part were issued on behalf of AAtW, neither they nor any of the pieces in the second part—to say nothing of this introduction—should be taken to represent a permanent, collective ideological position of the group as a whole. For better or worse, AAtW is a pragmatic action initiative with no ideological platform, no manifesto, and no program for the future of the region. As the introduction to our 2007 zine states,

> AAtW sweats off the excess weight of thick, heavy ideological frames by making *practice* its center

of gravity. This is not to imply that principled, theoretical analyses are not needed, of course—we certainly encourage applying them to deconstruct Zionist apartheid myths; however, at this time, the individuals comprising AAtW would rather apply tugging ropes, bolt cutters, and ten-pound hammers to deconstruct Israel's wall and express their disagreement with IDF roadblocks.

While many Israelis who participate in actions in the West Bank do hold some variety of a comprehensive anarchist worldview, many others do not. Some see their efforts in terms of support for human rights and international law. Others act out of a purely personal expression of moral conscience. This diversity has not been without its pitfalls, but one of its clear advantages has been the avoidance of sectarianism and corresponding ability to offer a slightly more welcoming space to newcomers. In short, the pieces collected here solely represent the opinions of their own authors.

In closing, we would like to thank the following Institute for Anarchist Studies board members: Joshua Stephens for taking the initiative to make this book happen and his substantial editorial help, Cindy Milstein for her careful copyediting, and Josh MacPhee (also with Justseeds Artists' Cooperative) for patiently going through numerous revisions of the cover art. We also want to acknowledge Lorna Vetters for proofreading this book. And we thank all the contributors who have dedicated their time and energy to writing and editing.

This book is dedicated to the memory of our fallen Palestinian comrades in the popular struggle against the occupation.

—Uri Gordon and Ohal Grietzer

STATEMENTS
AND SPEECHES

First Announcement

This press release was issued on December 25, 2003, during the action in which Gil Na'amati was shot, but before details of his injury were known.

No to the ghetto that's being built by Jews!
No to walls between people!
Stop the occupation!
Israelis, Palestinians, and international activists!
Bring down the apartheid wall in Mas'ha!

At this moment, Friday afternoon (seventh candle of Hanukkah), dozens of activists are tearing apart and breaking down the gate of the apartheid wall, which is also known as the "separation fence," to enable free passage for the people of Mas'ha to their lands. The activists, equipped with tools, are breaking through the gate that has remained closed since the wall was built two months ago. The farmers, whose land is on the other side of the fence, were told that they would be able to cross through the gate to work their lands. That promise turned out to be a methodical, crude, and cruel lie. All along the suffocating wall, the gates remain blocked and the Palestinian residents remain with no access to their only source of income.

The army is present at the Mas'ha village gates, which are located next to the Elkana settlement, and yet it is not clear how the confrontation between the army and the activists will end. The activists are calling for joint active resistance by Israelis and Palestinians against the ghettoizing policy that the Israeli government is pursuing.

The action is being held as a part of the Alternative Protest Camp against the Apartheid Wall that started a week ago in Deir Balut. The camp hosts Israelis and Palestinians, and is located on the path of the apartheid wall, on the land of the village's elementary school. (The building of the school was stopped due to the land being confiscated for the building of the wall.)

We invite the media that follows Ariel Sharon's promises for the so-called evacuation of the settlements to come and see for themselves the land confiscation and settlement expansion operation that is taking place these days. Deir Balut protest camp and other protest actions that are taking place, and that will take place in the future, will provide a living and kicking alternative to the occupying, stealing, and confiscating actions that the Sharon government and the Israeli army are responsible for.

—Anarchists Against the Wall

Declaration

This declaration was first released on January 5, 2004.

These days, with the building of the system of fences, ditches, and the wall of separation that robs the fields and leaves people in enclaves without the necessary means of existence, when hundreds of thousands are cut off from health and education facilities and essential infrastructure, and are forced to choose between "voluntary" transfer or death, it is our duty as human beings to struggle against this crime.

We forced open the gate at Mas'ha to open a gap in the wall of hatred, and with our actions, provide a living, kicking alternative to the apartheid policy of the Israeli government. We, to whom the future of this land is important, regard the system of fences and a separation wall as not only a huge disaster for the Palestinian people but also a direct threat for us and anyone who desires a peaceful as well as secure life. This is not a security fence. This is a racist apartheid fence that will cause bloodshed for all of us for many years to come. We try to live in our daily lives the changes we are striving for. We work in a spirit of full cooperation, without leaders. Our decisions are arrived at by consensus, and everyone contributes according to their ability. We believe that justice and equality are arrived at by voluntary agreement between people, and that the state is only an aggressive tool of dominant ethnic and/or class groups.

We are realists and understand that the abolition of the state system will not occur tomorrow, but even today we can already demand a way of life with "no rulers and no ruled," "no masters and no slaves." Direct action is the democratic act when democracy stops functioning. The Berlin wall was not dismantled by rulers and agreements but rather by citizens who felled it with their own hands.

Since we can remember, we have been brainwashed with hatred and fear of our Palestinian neighbors. We have not gone for trips in the countryside without armed escort. We were told that our hand is extended for peace, but there is no one to talk to. But these lies were exposed and are visible to everyone who participates in the actions against the occupation. We have slept together beneath the olive trees (before they were uprooted), we have marched together to the fence, and we will continue to struggle together—Israelis, Palestinians, and internationals—for justice and equality for all.

For years, good people have claimed that when the transfer is enacted, they will lie down in front of the wheels of the trucks and buses to block that crime. But the transfer is already happening now! Depriving thousands of people of the minimal means of existence does not leave them any alternative. Thousands are leaving their villages to find food for their children. The ethnic cleansing is occurring before our eyes, and we have only one option: to use the few rights we still have from the remnants of Israeli democracy and break the racist, immoral laws. Yes, to break the gates and fences, block the bulldozers with our bodies, enter closed-off military areas, and also transform the enemy into our friend. Palestinian and Israeli resistance will continue as long as the occupation—the infrastructure and root of terror—continues.

—Anarchists Against the Wall

Two States for Two Peoples— Two States Too Many

The following leaflet was distributed at a demonstration in Tel Aviv on May 15, 2004. The short-lived Anarchist-Communist Initiative was formed by a small group of Israeli anarchists, some of whom were imprisoned for refusing to serve in the army, from three different cities.

If the state of Israel and Palestinian Authority reach a "peace" agreement, it will not result from an Israeli wish for "security" for its citizens and a Palestinian wish for "independence." It will be—more than anything else—a part of the configuration of the international powers' interests, as such concepts are alien to their way of thinking. The Geneva Accords, initiated by politicians and business-people if signed and applied as intended (two different things), will be the expression of these interests, as will any other political agreement one can imagine. The label most appropriate for describing the treatment by the Israeli state of the inhabitants and citizens who are not included in the

category of "full-rights Jews" is *apartheid*: a chauvinist separation rule, which confiscates land from peasants, restricts
the freedom of movement of people on their way to work,
and even obstructs the ability of Palestinian capitalists to
develop their economy. All this, while trying to get the cooperation of the Palestinian leadership.

Some people who regard themselves as peace activists have asked themselves seriously, beyond the official
answers of the Left, what the reasons for the common
policy of all Israeli governments—left and right—toward
the Palestinians can be? We claim that it is not simply the
conquering of one people by another, in the style of ancient
empires; nor just the expression of a belief in an undi-
vided Land of Israel drawn from the Bible; neither does it
stem from pressure from a strong lobby of settlers' leaders,
though that surely plays a role too.

The apartheid rule must be seen as something that
serves several powerful interests. First, it serves the Israeli
economy—meaning the Israeli capitalists—by supplying
cheap labor power, which is mainly used by small and
medium-size employers in manufacturing and construction.

The "Israeli Arabs" who were under military rule during the years 1948 to 1966 have played this role, and even
more so, the inhabitants of the regions occupied in 1967.
Only lately, as if it were a result of the Al-Aqsa Intifada and
massive "importation" of temporary work immigrants, was
free access to that labor interrupted. Big Israeli compa-
nies profited from the 1967 occupation mainly because
it opened up a large consumer market for them with no
competitors. The military establishment, which has always

been powerful in Israel, and its top personnel have always enjoyed sure careers in government and industry after finishing their military service, and have a vested interest in prolonging the apartheid (and conflict) in order to assure their position as well as rights. It is in the interest of the United States, which is helped by the services given to it by the Israeli state in the region and all over the world since the 1950s, for Israel to stay under a permanent threat so that it will continue to need its support.

A reminder: serious talks about the establishment of a Palestinian state only started fifteen years ago, toward the end of the first Intifada. Hardly any present-day leaders of the main Zionist Left and more radical Left (which seems to have succeeded in rewriting its history in an almost Orwellian manner) ever imagined such an agreement. Even at the beginning of the Oslo period they still talked about autonomy. The Palestinian Liberation Organization and anti-Zionist Left were talking about the establishment of a secular state of all its citizens. The Palestinian Authority did not exist at all, in fact, until Israel helped to establish the Palestinian Liberation Organization in this role. The peace agreement providing for two states for two nations only entered the agenda when, following the first Intifada and changes in the global world economy, it began to fit the interests of sections of Israeli and US capital.

What does such a peace mean? If we continue the description of the situation in extended Israel as apartheid and compare it to that which existed in South Africa, we can see that *peace* means the submission of the Intifada to a comprador Palestinian leadership that will serve Israel.

Such peace, often called "normalization," is related to processes occurring all over the world under the label of globalization and initiatives for regional trade cooperation designed to culminate in a "free trade region of all Mediterranean countries." All over the world, agreements such as these have led to the takeover of local economies by multinational concerns, the infringement of basic human rights, deterioration in the status and conditions of women and children, social violence, and the destruction of the environment.

Will such an agreement and peace at least bring the cessation of violence? We do not think so: economic hardship and social gaps will increase, the refugee problem will remain unsolved, and the international economic support given to the huge number of unemployed in the Gaza Strip and parts of the West Bank will be legitimated (as partly happened after the Oslo Agreement and again more recently). In this case, Palestinians will have to rely on "their" state—a small, dependent ministate unlikely to be up to the task.

States act within a system of interests, and common people like us are not high on their list of concerns. If we want to bring about any sort of change for the better, to decrease the gaps and stop the mutual killing, we need to behave not as the obedient puppets of political leaders financed by Europeans and Americans who do nothing more than the odd "democratic" protest. We need to act instead in order to remove national partitions, and above all resist the military forces that cause mutual and continuous slaughter.

We do not need to promote a political program, be it that of the Geneva Accords or some alternative. Rather, we must put the demand for an entirely different way of life and equality for all the inhabitants of the region on the agenda. Even if we act in an independent (local) way, we still have to remember that as long as there are states and as long as the capitalist system continues to exist, every improvement we manage to achieve will be partial and under permanent threat. Thus, we have to see our struggle as part of the struggle being carried on throughout the whole world against global capitalism, call for a revolutionary change based on the abolition of class oppression and exploitation, and aim toward building a new society—a classless anarchist-communist society. A society in which there will be no state coercion, where organized violence will be abolished, where chauvinism will be nonexistent, and where all other evils of the capitalist era will be removed.

—Anarchist-Communist Initiative

We Must Break Down the Wall!

Leaflet distributed on September 23, 2004, in Tel Aviv during the celebrations for the release of five Israeli conscientious objectors after two years in prison.

Would you buy a used toaster from Dani Nave [Israeli government minister]? Would you buy a used car from Tsahi Hanegby [another Israeli government minister]? So how come you buy these disastrous plans that will influence your life for many years to come from them and their friends, Arik, Bibi, Ehud, and Limor, along with all the other interested parties from everywhere on up to the Likud Central Committee?

DO YOU TRUST THEM THAT THE SOLUTION HERE IS FENCES, WALLS, AND APARTHEID?

At the end of 2002, the Israeli government started to build a separation fence. The route decided on mostly passes deep within the Palestinian area, destroying thousands of acres of agricultural land, separating children from their schools, sick people from their medical treatment, and people from their relatives. The twisted route creates ghettos—enclaves that prevent normal connections between villages and the surrounding world. Thousands of fruit trees are being uprooted to clear the way—trees that provide the main source of income to people who are already prevented from working in Israel. The government presents the route as just a security measure, but both the Israeli Supreme Court and International Court of Justice have stated that the route is illegal and seriously harms the lives of the inhabitants. This raises the questions: "Was this harsh harming of the inhabitants taken into the security considerations? Does a person whose resources have been stolen, whose trees have been uprooted and whose honor has been trampled become less dangerous?"

So if it is not for security, what really hides behind the decision to build such a fence? The sad answer is *transfer*. Not the kind in which people are forced on to transports and taken away but instead a quiet transfer—one where life is made so unbearable for people that they are left with only two options: to get out or explode.

Since January 2004, the villagers have chosen a different option: nonviolent struggle against the fence inspired by figures like Nelson Mandela and Martin Luther King Jr. Men, women, children, and old people go out of the villages to try to block the bulldozers with their bodies, to prevent the destruction and robbery, accompanied by Israeli and international activists who arrived to stand by their side in solidarity and try to decrease the level of violence of the army. This was not always helpful. Frequently the army responds with extreme violence using batons, shock and tear gas grenades, rubber-coated bullets, and even live ammunition. Throughout the year there have been dozens of harshly repressed demonstrations, resulting in the killing of six demonstrators and the injury of hundreds. The media has usually chosen not to focus on what's happening, and only a decision from the Supreme Court stopped the free stampede of bulldozers for a while. In recent days, work on the building of the fence has been renewed with full speed, again in the Palestinian areas, in clear disregard for the Supreme Court's verdicts. Now it is no longer possible to avert your eyes and say, "We did not know."

NOW IS THE TIME TO ACT!
STOP THE MADNESS!
STOP THE FENCE!

—Anarchists Against the Wall

The Carl von Ossietzky Medal Acceptance Speech

On December 7, 2008, in Berlin, the Bil'in Popular Committee and AAtW were jointly awarded the prestigious Carl von Ossietzky Medal, given annually by the International League of Human Rights and named after the German Nobel Peace Prize winner who died in Gestapo custody.

We would like to be honest—we are standing here, at this podium, although as anarchists this situation raises mixed feelings for us as well as our comrades. Honestly, we are reluctant to receive prizes for political activism. We would prefer not to be singled out for glory and receive gratitude for doing what we feel is our duty. Despite our anarchist reservations, which under normal circumstances would have prevailed, as Israelis and beneficiaries of our country's unjust deeds toward Palestinians, we are thankful for your support of the Palestinian struggle against Israeli apartheid.

Here at this podium, just as in the olive groves of the West Bank, our primary moral duty is not to maintain ideological purity but rather to stand with Palestinians in their resistance to oppression. We recognize the importance of garnering international support for the ongoing struggle and the major contribution of this award to this end. We believe that standing here, in the current state of affairs, is a direct continuation of the blocking of bulldozers, standing side by side with the stone throwers, or running away from tear gas along with young and elderly protesters.

Here, as in the olive groves, we would like to stress that we are not equal partners but rather occupiers who join the occupied in *their* struggle. We are aware of the fact that for many, the participation of Israelis in a Palestinian struggle serves as a stamp of approval, but in our eyes, this partnership is not about granting legitimacy. The Palestinian struggle is legitimate with or without us. Instead, the struggle is an opportunity for us to cross, in action rather than words, the barriers of national allegiance.

Over the past four years, and through over two hundred demonstrations, Bil'in has become a symbol and focal point for the movement against Israel's wall—a movement that for the past six years has mobilized thousands of people into grassroots popular resistance and forged an unprecedented on-the-ground, joint Palestinian-Israeli struggle.

The fact that the movement is a civilian and unarmed one only serves to accentuate the army's excessive and unjust violence. Thousands have been injured, hundreds jailed and imprisoned for lengthy periods, and fifteen were killed—ten of them minors. We would like to dedicate this medal to the two most recent casualties of the struggle: ten-year-old Ahmad Mousa and seventeen-year-old Youssef Amirah, who were murdered by border police officers in the village of Ni'ilin four months ago as part of the attempt to militarily suppress the wall-related insurrection in the village.

Thank you again for supporting the joint popular struggle.

—Adi Winter and Yossi Bartal
Anarchists Against the Wall

Speech at the Tel Aviv Demo against the War in Gaza

On January 3, 2009, eight days after the beginning of Operation Cast Lead, AAtW took part in a one-thousand-person-strong march and rally in Tel Aviv against the attack on Gaza. The following is the speech that two AAtW members wrote for the event.

The attacks on Gaza bear witness to an alarming process pushing Israeli society further into the realms of extremism. Through this process, attacks on civilian populations become more and more brutal, while being simultaneously portrayed as essential—in fact, as the epitome of justice. It is the process of a moral obtuseness washing over our entire society—a process by which everything and anything becomes permissible.

What makes this extremism possible? It takes hold through the distortion of facts and blurring of notions. Such blurring is encouraged and nurtured by politicians and military officials, and it has been accompanying us as a society for a long time. We can all recall how the deepening of the occupation in Gaza and the West Bank was referred to as a peace process, how total Israeli control over people's lives in Gaza was termed disengagement, and how a cruel siege that included mass starvation and withholding of the most basic goods became known as a period of "calm."

Today we are told that a ruthless attack on Gaza's populace is in fact a war on Hamas, dropping bombs on residential areas in the world's most densely populated region is not a war crime but instead "an assault on the infrastructure of terrorism," shelling the University of Gaza's female dorms is eliminating explosives labs, and murdering hundreds of women and children constitutes just and moral combat. Foreign Affairs Minister Tzipi Livni went even further and explained how waging war is essential to the advancement of peace, no less. Yes, it appears that what we are witnessing in Gaza today constitutes the Israeli government's current definition of a "peace process."

We have come here to say that this war is not necessary and is certainly not just. We have come here to refuse the politics of hatred and vengeance. We have come here to oppose the whitewashing of war crimes, and their portrayal as a fight against terrorists. We are here to say that those who speak out against civilian casualties in Sderot cannot avoid speaking out against the mass killing that is taking place in Gaza, courtesy of the Israeli army's bombardments.

Thousands of people, both Palestinian and Jewish, have demonstrated against the war in the course of the past week. Israel's security apparatus along with the mainstream media are doing their best to forcefully silence these voices of sanity. Those who expressed their opposition to the war were denounced as traitors, and their protests were portrayed as disturbances. But above all else, the prowar forces within Israel have tried to crush the growing dissent through mass arrests of Palestinians all across the country. Over seven hundred people who dared oppose the war have been arrested in the past week. More than two hundred of them are still imprisoned—nearly half of them minors. This is a form of racist, political persecution that should worry every single Israeli citizen.

We stand here today, together, Jews and Palestinians, women and men, to make sure our protest is heard, to say no to military attacks on civilian populations and no to war. We are frequently asked, Why are you constantly opposing? We are marching here today not to oppose but rather to voice our support: support for a cease-fire, for a period of real, mutual calm; support for lifting the siege, for recognition of the fact that Gaza and the West Bank are a single entity; support for an end to the occupation; and support for a joint Jewish-Palestinian struggle for liberty.

—Adar Grayevsky and Yanay Israeli
Anarchists Against the Wall

Sentencing Statement

On January 31, 2008, some thirty protesters participated in a Critical Mass bicycle ride in Tel Aviv to protest the siege of Gaza. During the protest, plainclothes police arrested Jonathan Pollak because they recognized him from previous protests, and as they claimed in court, assumed he was the organizer of and figurehead for the event. Jonathan read this statement before his sentencing.

Your Honor, once found guilty, it is then customary for the accused to ask the court for leniency and express remorse for having committed the offense. I find myself unable to do so, however. From its beginning, this trial contained practically no disagreements over the facts. As the indictment states, I indeed rode my bicycle, alongside others, through the streets of Tel Aviv to protest the siege on Gaza. And indeed, while riding our bicycles, which are legally vehicles that belong on the road, we may have slowed down traffic slightly. The sole, trivial disagreement in this case revolves around testimonies heard from police detectives who claimed I played a leading role throughout the protest bicycle ride—something I as well as the rest of the defense witnesses deny.

As said earlier, it is customary at this point of the proceedings to sound remorseful, and I would indeed like to voice my regrets regarding one particular aspect of that day's events: if there is remorse in my heart, it is that, just as I argued during the trial, I did not play a prominent role in the protest that day, and thus did not fulfill my duty to do everything within my power to change the unbearable situation of Gaza's inhabitants and bring to an end Israel's control over the Palestinians.

His Honor has stated during the court case, and will most likely state again in the future, that a trial is not a matter of politics but rather of law. To this I reply that there is hardly anything to this trial except political disagreement. This court may have impeded the mounting of an appropriate defense when it refused to hear arguments regarding political selectiveness in the police's conduct, but even from the testimonies that were admitted, it became clear that such selectiveness exists.

Both the subject of my alleged offense and the motivation behind it were political. This is something that cannot be sidestepped. The state of Israel maintains an illegitimate, inhuman, and illegal siege on the Gaza Strip, which still is occupied territory according to international law. This siege, carried out in my name and in yours as well, sir—in fact, in all our names—is a cruel collective punishment inflicted on ordinary citizens, residents of the Gaza strip, subjects without rights under Israeli occupation.

In the face of this reality, and as a stance against it, we chose on January 31, 2008, to exercise the freedom of speech afforded to Jewish citizens of Israel. Yet it appears that here in our one-of-many faux democracies in the Middle East, even this freedom is no longer granted, even to society's privileged children.

I am not surprised by the court's decision to convict me, despite having no doubt in my mind that our actions on that day correspond to the most basic, elementary definitions of a person's right to protest.

Indeed, as the prosecution pointed out, a suspended prison sentence hung over my head at the time of the bicycle protest, having been convicted before under an identical article of law. And although I still maintain I did not commit any offense whatsoever, I was aware of the possibility that under Israeli justice, my suspended sentence would be imposed.

I must add that if His Honor decides to go ahead and impose my suspended prison sentence, I will go to prison wholeheartedly and with my head held high. It will be the justice system itself, I believe, that ought to lower its eyes in the face of the suffering inflicted on Gaza's inhabitants, just like it lowers its eyes and averts its vision each and every day when faced with the realities of the occupation.

—Jonathan Pollak

ESSAYS AND REFLECTIONS

Nabi Saleh in Pictures

The road from Tel Aviv to Nabi Saleh is long and twisting, and the hills on the way were made for poetry. The five hundred residents of this small village, not far off from Ramallah, go out every Friday to protest against the Israeli occupation and the settlers who stole their spring. They march together, adults and children, accompanied by international and Israeli solidarity activists, to confront the soldiers who are always out there blocking their way to the spring.

◆

We're standing in the main square of the village as people gather up for the demonstration. It's my first time in Nabi Saleh, and I am more than a little bit scared. Most of what I have heard about the village was in first aid classes, so I know all about the different sorts of injuries to be expected, but nothing about the people. Bassem Tamimi walks over and introduces himself. His warm welcome will cross my mind whenever I see his face in photos from the military court and prison afterward.

As we start marching, Tal tells me about the protests and shows me escape routes. She is cut off abruptly by a rain of tear gas canisters, putting those escape routes into immediate use. We march again. This time instead of the whooshing sound of the canisters, we hear the "pak pak" made by bullets. She tells me, "Rubber," and we start running. As we stand panting behind a conveniently located house, we look at each other and admit, "Those were live bullets." Welcome to Nabi Saleh.

◆

It's the end of winter. The army has blocked all the roads to Nabi Saleh, so we walk through the fields and climb the hill that leads to the village. The flowers are blooming in yellow and red and purple, and with all this beauty around the purpose of this trip is momentarily forgotten. But as we get to the village, the soldiers are already inside and there is gas in the main square.

◆

Pouring rain, real rain for a change. We are taking shelter in one of the houses as a girl comes in and screams, "They took Uday." We all rush outside. In the square, a military jeep is standing. Uday is sitting inside. There are soldiers all around. Two dozen of us sit in front of the jeep, blocking its way. After several minutes the soldiers say, "Anybody who doesn't move along will be arrested." We remain sitting. The ground is wet, and the little kids of the village come and offer us pieces of cardboard cut off boxes that we can sit on. We squeeze on to them. A soldier points at one of the activists they know well, and tells the other, "That's Kobi, take him, you can arrest him any day." So they come

and take him. He doesn't resist, although some of us do try
to get in the way. When they try to grab the girl who sat
next to him, though, they pepper spray her and all those
who try to de-arrest her. As people are lying on the floor,
clutching their faces and screaming in pain, the soldiers
start shooting tear gas. While we busy ourselves with tend-
ing to the injured, the military jeep drives off, carrying away
two Israeli arrestees, along with sixteen-year-old Uday. The
Israelis were released that very day. For Uday, it took another eight months.

◆

The soldiers are blocking the protest. Several dozens of
us stand in front of them. Hurriyah is leading the chants.
She stands as close as she can get to the soldier opposing
her. "Ihtilal!" she chants. "Thawra!" we answer. "Istitan!"
"Thawra!" "al Jidar!" "Thawra!" To the words "occupation,"
"settlements," and "the wall," we offer the same response,
"revolution." For a long time the chants go on and on, until
a soldier drops a gas canister in our midst, and the group
breaks up in its haste to get away. I hide behind the fence
of a nearby house, on the same line with the soldiers. They
won't gas this area. Then I go back and along with another friend start yelling at them, "Does that make you feel
brave?" "Do you feel like heroes?" "Much respect, you succeeded in dispersing a group of people who were shouting
slogans," and so on. Two little girls are walking back down
the road. They stop when they reach the soldiers. They start
singing. "Mawtini, Mawtini," they sing. "My homeland, my
homeland," the Palestinian anthem, two six-year-old girls

chime in front of a dozen fully armed soldiers. They sing in small childish voices, but their words ring loud and clear, and from behind them more and more people start coming, until the whole group that was dispersed by gas stands there echoing, "Mawtini." When the song is over, the group breaks into another one, and another one follows. It took a blue spray of smelly skunk water from the army's cannon to put an end to the singing and send everybody running again. In the air, the voices remained.

◆

I'm sitting in a café in Tel Aviv with some friends. We have chosen to spend this Friday in Tel Aviv in order to hold banners for the boycott, divestment, and sanctions campaign at the human rights march. In between sandwiches and coffee, I'm following the tweets from Nabi Saleh on my phone. Tear gas canisters shot directly at protesters, rubber bullets, minor injuries, nothing out of the ordinary. All of a sudden, though, there is twitter hysteria. "Someone was critically injured in Nabi." I tell my friends. I'm reading the tweets out loud. They say head injury, they say directly hit by a tear gas canister from a short distance, they say Mustafa Tamimi and blood everywhere. They don't leave much place for hope. I can hear them screaming through my smartphone screen, I can see the blood, and there's nothing I can do but share the information, and pray, but I've got nothing to pray to.

I'm pretty sure I've made some plans for the evening. I can't recall what they were. I'm supposed to be writing my coursework; instead I'm writing Facebook updates and reading tweets. I follow the updates throughout the Friday meal with my family, and I sit in front of the computer late into the night. As the evening proceeds it looks like there is some reason for optimism. The reports from the hospital say that it looks like he is going to make it, with no brain damage, and they might even save his eye. Looking at his injury photo on Facebook, though, it seems quite unlikely, but I want to believe it. I go to sleep to the sounds of Leonard Cohen singing "Hallelujah," the only prayer I know. The morning comes, I reach out for my phone, and the first tweet I see says it all: "Martyr Mustafa Tamimi." My eyes are not fully open yet, but they are already full of tears.

◆

We join in the funeral procession. There are flags and there are slogans as it makes its way toward the village, but there are mainly tears. A woman faints. People walk and hold on to one another. Everybody seems so . . . broken. My pain is mingled with anger, my anger drowned in pain. I want to burn something—preferably my Israeli ID. I want nothing to do with the people who did it, with the people who killed Mustafa, with the people who broke my beloved village. I leave a piece of my heart in the graveyard of Nabi Saleh, lying beside Mustafa Tamimi.

When the funeral is over, people start marching on the more familiar route. The Shabab lead the way toward the spring, and everybody follows. Friday or Sunday, protest or funeral, the soldiers react the same way. Soon enough the tear gas fills the air, the eyes are tearful again, and the wind carries the smell of the skunk water toward the village.

We have to go home. Before we leave, I walk toward
Mustafa's to offer my condolences to Ikhlas, his mother.
A car stops by the house. Inside it sits Uday, Mustafa's
brother, who was in prison since that demonstration way
back when. The military court agreed to release him a few
days earlier than his due date because of his brother's death,
but releasing him in time for the funeral would have been
too kind for them. As he walks out he falls into the arms
of Louai, his twin, both weeping uncontrollably. I follow
them into the house, but when Ikhlas hugs Uday and starts
crying into his shoulder, I walk away. I don't want to in-
trude, and anyway, I have no idea what to say.

◆

It's my first Friday in the village since Mustafa's funeral, and
it's the Friday after Christmas. We run into Bilal's house
and close the door just in time to lock out the cloud of gas
that's been chasing us. Ma'ath and I sit together, and update
on twitter, while waiting for the air outside to clear so we
can rejoin the protest. Seven-year-old Jana walks around
the house ringing a Christmas bell and begs her mum for
permission to dress up in her Santa outfit. She gets to wear
the jacket only and the beard. She skips around the house,
ringing her bell, singing merrily, "Bombing gas, bombing
gas, bombing all the way, bombing gas, bombing gas, on
this Christmas Day, yay," and we are not sure whether our
hearts are bursting or breaking.

◆

I am sitting at a friend's place trying to read books for my seminar. I'm in the midst of one Internet break. It's been a bad Sunday. Soldiers took Bilal on Friday, and hopes for his release seem scarce. It seems like there's nothing but bad news all around. But then I see a photo. A photo of Palestinian women sitting by the Nabi Saleh spring, and the caption by Abir Kopty says, "For the first time in two years, a group of Palestinian women went to the spring of Nabi Saleh and spent their day there. The spring was taken over by settlers two years ago under the protection of the army and state. Viva Palestine and Palestinian women!" Suddenly the day has grown brighter, and the weight on my shoulders has eased. And once again, the women of Nabi Saleh teach me hope.

—Leehee Rothschild

Tear Gas and Tea

The truly marginalized political positions belong in a category of ideas that are considered mad or irresponsible. The former label usually requires no argument, but the latter is supported by a contention that cannot be dismissed out of hand. As the assertion goes, when a position is sufficiently marginalized it actually becomes counterproductive. Instead, the responsible mad person is urged toward the often-contradictory responsible position. This urging is possible when the basic terms of discussion are sufficiently distorted, and therefore it is useful to take another look at them.

When the Antiracist Is Incomprehensible

Israel has all but completed what it calls a security barrier (the wall) in the West Bank. The impact of this, the largest construction project in Israeli history, can only be understood in connection with the range of other Israeli policies and practices in the West Bank—dozens of staffed checkpoints, literally hundreds of physical barriers, and policies of closure and curfew. Together, they enforce an elaborate system of restrictions on the movement of all Palestinians in accordance with ever-changing rules that are not published, and thus are almost impossible to challenge legally. These policies and others divide the Palestinian territories into what is called "territorial units" in IDF lingo. More than any previous Israeli policy or practice, the wall, if completed according to plan, stands to make the partition of the West Bank permanent and irreversible.

The spectrum of Israeli opposition to the wall, from liberals to radicals, falls into three main categories. The first category, the principled position, is to oppose the wall on the grounds that it is a policy that punishes people for being Palestinian. Its alternative, the second category, opposes the wall on the grounds that it is not an efficient way to achieve its stated goal of protecting Israelis, either because it does not provide security or because a more humane wall could offer an equal amount of security. These two categories are diametrically opposed in the sense that to criticize the wall for being inefficient is to imply that had the wall been efficient, it would have been legitimate. The third category is a variation on the second. It contains calls for the construction of the wall on the green line, but crucially omits the condition that Israel retreat back to the green line. This position is the common one on the Israeli Center-Left and is part of the platform of Meretz—the Israeli social democratic party.

The difference between the first and third position is more than a matter of the unintended consequent route of the wall. Without an Israeli withdrawal from the West Bank, even if the wall had been built on the green line as Meretz wished, it would have facilitated the caging of

Palestinians by other means. With the Israeli army remaining on both sides of the wall, freedom of movement for Palestinians could have remained increasingly constrained by checkpoints, restricted roads, and internal fences. Such tight control would not have been possible without a wall preventing Palestinian access to Israel, even if that wall was on the green line.

To my knowledge, principled opposition to the wall has not been expressed in the Israeli press at all, and rarely even in statements of the radical Left. The dilemma for Israeli radicals facing a tide of support for the wall is between making an inherently racist argument and risking their exclusion from the mainstream.

To further illustrate what it means to even criticize the wall on any grounds other than a principled opposition, consider the reaction to the idea of imposing on Jews a regime similar to that imposed on Palestinians. The scale of reaction to that hypothetical suggestion can be measured by the response to a related restriction proposed for the Jewish state. That proposal is UN Security Council Resolution 242, which, if implemented, would prevent the Jewish state from ruling over Palestinians in the occupied territories. Israel's Foreign Minister Abba Eban responded to Resolution 242 by stating, "We have openly said that the map will never again be the same as on June 4, 1967. For us, this is a matter of security and of principles. The June map is for us equivalent to insecurity and danger. I do not exaggerate when I say that it has for us something of a memory of Auschwitz." Following Eban, the Israeli Right commonly refers to the 1967 borders of Israel as "Auschwitz borders."

Moreover, consider the idea that restrictions on Jews would be justified by the existence of a "Jewish threat." Such a discussion should be rejected flat out, in its entirety, as being extremely racist. Claiming that a so-called Jewish threat could be dealt with differently would undermine such an unequivocal rejection. In fact, even the mere allusion to a Jewish threat in terms such as "Jewish Bolshevism" portrays those using it as anti-Semitic. Thus, to continue arguing for a more efficient way to deal with such a threat is to accept one of two racist premises that may underlie it—namely, that all Jews are responsible for the actions of some Jews, or that even if they are not, it is still legitimate to punish innocent Jews. The first of these premises is the official position of the state of Israel, whose leaders have repeatedly declared that the Jewish state belongs not just to its citizens but also to the Jewish people as a whole. Only those who are considered immune from charges of anti-Semitism can make such a statement. Otherwise, these terms would be rejected and condemned.

This reaction should be kept in mind when it comes to racism against Arabs. To take just one of countless examples, it is apparently acceptable for a major Israeli newspaper to title the cover story of its weekend section "The Bedouin Threat" in large red letters over a picture of young children at a dump site. Furthermore, while a discussion of Jewish Bolshevism is immediately understood as racist due to its implication of all Jews, the same treatment is not meted out to the widely used term "Islamic Terrorism." The almost-universal acceptance of such racist phrases is the reason why opposing the wall on principled grounds is either incomprehensible in the Israeli media or seen as an endorsement of the murder of Israelis. Israelis opposed to the wall often argue along the lines of the alternative to the principled position. Yet when they do so, it is a concession to the racist assumption underlying that notion.

Dilemmas of Privilege

Media work and, to a lesser extent, other appeals to the public present a dilemma between opposing the wall on principled and marginalized grounds, or conceding to the racist assumptions underlying the alternatives. Naturally, interaction with other Israeli institutions ranging from the Israeli High Court of Justice to infantry troops present parallel predicaments.

In several instances, in what might seem like a victory, the High Court ordered that the route of the wall be changed. Almost without exception, these decisions also set precedents that legitimized much larger sections of the wall. Regardless of the effect on the wall, an appeal to a court that approved the execution of Palestinians without trial is a repulsive concession. An appeal to the court also might provide false hopes and defuse an otherwise more militant popular struggle. In spite of this, Palestinians who were directly impacted by the wall filed dozens of appeals to the High Court.

It is not hard to understand how a similar dilemma exists with respect to contacts with other levels of Israeli officials or soldiers. For example, it is frequently possible for activists (especially Israelis) to engage in a form of on-the-spot negotiations with soldiers about minor "concessions," such as being granted permission to demonstrate at a certain location. On the one hand, such negotiations might reduce the physical risk to demonstrators or buy some time; on the other hand, the act of negotiating recognizes the army's authority as well as offering a pretext for attacking the demonstration when the "agreement" is not kept. As above, the process of negotiation also serves to defuse the momentum of a demonstration or march.

What is less widely accepted is the fact that the same sort of difficulty exists even in the cooperation between Palestinian and Israeli activists in the West Bank. The privileged position of Israelis means, for instance, that they have greater access to the media and the ability to move much more freely, in addition to facing much lower legal and physical risk. This tends to increase the influence that Israelis have on decisions about a struggle that affects their Palestinian counterparts considerably more. In other words, even when using Israeli privilege for the purpose of the struggle there is a concession. That is to say, in a sense, the privilege is extended in the struggle as well.

Even social interaction can extend Israeli privilege. The relative freedom of Israelis elevates their social position, and social ties created under these conditions reflect that, thereby perpetuating privilege. At least to some degree, this applies even to the social ties between Israeli and Palestinian activists. This phenomenon is one facet of what is referred to in Palestinian society as "normalization." As I see it, this term means that any interaction that Palestinians carry out with Israelis, be it for the most positive purpose, while the conditions are such that Israel occupies Palestine, contains within it a degree of adjustment to these conditions and, in a way, even their extension. This sensitivity is partly a result of the fact that some of the most damaging Israeli policies were described as confidence-building measures or similar processes, accompanied by promises of Israeli good intentions.

There is a contrasting idea, which is that interaction between Israelis and Palestinians—and in particular, social interaction—can eliminate mutual fear and suspicion—supposedly the root cause of the conflict. Another variation on this idea, one that I find more realistic, is that social interactions are valuable because they strengthen the basis for a joint struggle. The value, even the very justification, of joint political action should be weighed with this in mind. The question is perhaps illustrated in the choice that Israelis make when coming to the West Bank: whether to drink tea or inhale tear gas at a demonstration.

A member of the Popular Committee Against the Wall in the Palestinian village of Bil'in expresses a sentiment that is perhaps unappreciated in the wider circles of Israeli activists. His message to Israelis is, "After we end the occupation together, there will be plenty of time for tea."

The Choice of Satanists

In Israel, like many other societies, the term "anarchist" is commonly used in a derogatory manner, and its most accurate synonym is probably "Satanist." The satanic association actually serves two purposes: it frees AAtW from considerations of its public image, which tends to paralyze political action, and more important, it demonstrates the group's intent to set its own agenda. This in turn strengthens the group, as it offers its members and potential members the option to act according to their honest opinion, as opposed to taking a compromised position in a debate whose terms are dictated by others.

Another unique aspect of AAtW's work is the joint struggle it wages together with Palestinians. This, of course, is not without its difficulties. It is hard to expect Palestinians to immediately accept and trust Israelis. In addition to the fear of spies and provocateurs, cooperation with Israelis also involves an element of normalization: an adjustment to the conditions of the occupation. Israeli activists also bring with them cultural influences that might not be welcome in some parts of Palestinian society. In light of this, and although it has no formalized ideological platform, AAtW does insist on several principles of joint work. The first principle is that although the struggle is joint, Palestinians are affected more by the decisions taken within it, and therefore are the ones who should make the important decisions. Second, Israelis have a special responsibility to respect Palestinian self-determination, including respecting social customs and keeping out of internal Palestinian politics.

Weighing the negative aspects of normalization versus the benefits of social ties is a harder question. Unlike cultural standards such as modest behavior and dress, it would be far more repressive to try to codify what constitutes appropriate social ties, let alone demand it of individuals. The only principle is the general policy of respecting requests by Palestinian popular committees in this regard as well.

All of this might give the impression that the difficulties in a joint struggle are larger than they really are. Instead, the joint struggle faces only one main problem: the Israeli state. The attention given to the issues above is meant to highlight the process of political development that AAtW has gone through together with its Palestinian partners. Over years of intense struggle, at certain low points the above dilemmas came to the surface and had to be dealt with. As perhaps the main contact between the Israeli and Palestinian peace movements, AAtW transmitted its experience to the Israeli peace movement and played a key role in its political development. At the time of AAtW's beginning, the idea of Israelis joining Palestinian demonstrations seemed incredible to the huge majority of the Israeli Left. After several years of activity, the number of Israelis who have themselves participated in joint demonstrations with Palestinians is in the thousands, and includes many who are personally not marginalized at all. Still, other than political parties with a mostly Arab constituency, no Israeli political party has supported the joint struggle against the wall.

The obligation of citizens to resist criminal acts and policies carried out by their government is recognized in international law, and requires Israelis to do all they can to resist their government. More important, the moral obligation of resisting the wall becomes apparent to anyone who has witnessed it cutting off villages and towns, or merely seen its path drawn on a map. To look away and ignore the crimes committed in our names, with our taxes, by the students we train or those we keep polite company with, is to lose part of one's humanity. This is a burden that Israelis are enslaved to by fear. In that sense, the act of disobedience and resistance is also an act of personal liberation—an option open to all Israelis who would join the struggle. The struggle of Palestinians against those who would have them move away or disappear is a constant struggle to simply exist. Israeli supporters join this struggle one day at a time, at a certain risk to themselves. Nevertheless, the harshest penalty likely for Israelis does not include a lifetime of financial insecurity and being subjected to the whims of occupying soldiers. If those penalties are not enough to deter our Palestinian partners, they should not deter us Israelis either.

—Kobi Snitz

Fear and Loathing at the Central Bus Station

think Tel Aviv is not only the most beautiful city on the face of the earth; it's probably also the most beautiful city that could ever possibly be. But that's a minority opinion. Activists tend to think of it and everything around it, and of Israel in general, as despicably heinous. They are right, of course: wherever you go, you're surrounded by soldiers.

Soldiers in uniform carrying guns. Reserve soldiers, living their civilian lives, except for one month a year, when they go back to being proper soldiers. Former soldiers, who think you too should be a soldier. Mothers, fathers, wives of soldiers. People who think that soldiers are always right, and that they deserve a 10 percent discount in shawarma stands, and that they keep us safe. Border police soldiers on civil police duty. Oh, and there's that depressed, alienated, self-loathing little soldier that I used to be.

And since soldiers are not only the people doing wrong but also those who might arrest you, or shoot you, or kill your friend this coming Friday, you don't just dislike them, you're also scared. Days spent feeling surrounded, wishing you were anywhere else. Ending up in school in Berlin or somewhere up the East Coast.

Little communities protect us from the world of soldiers. Being vegan helps make the cut clear. Veganarchism doesn't just mean not feeding off the suffering of animals; like orthodox Judaism, it also means not eating with the gen pop of the barracks of Isra-hell. With the infoshop, and the vegan-queer-punk-cult bar, and a couple of semicommunes, we almost have what it takes to keep apart at times. We can't avoid the increasingly rampant fascism and capitalism, but we have our hideouts when we need them.

You can't reason with the people who defend soldiers. They're totally brainwashed. Facts don't matter; my stance just can't make sense on their terms. That Jews are an oppressed, hunted, endangered species is for them an uncontestable, elementary truth. That to survive, us Jews must strike—strike hard and first—is what we're taught since we're old enough to be taught anything at all. And it always comes down to that, and so details like whose land the wall cuts through, and who said what in court, and who it was that cast some stone or shot some bullet, and at whom— are nothing anyone really should, at bottom, ever mind.

So we give up on these people. Our statements are not meant to communicate but to rage and keep us going. The slogans at our demos, from a Zionist outside, appear as the expression of a world turned upside down, self-hating and senseless. With no audience, the demos make little sense to us as well. I never chanted slogans with any genuine passion until I shouted them from within a fascist mock block, and never have I sung a song of protest with such fervor as I did

"Hatikva" wearing a fascist-chic black shirt and a red band around my arm. AAtW's most spectacular action was a die-in during the attack on Gaza. Finally, we embraced the explicit wish of those so glad to see civilians bombarded (no, not civilians—terrorists, terrorist supporters, and kids who will grow up to be terrorists): the wish that the anarchist traitors would just drop dead.

◆

My own activism was first sparked by Einat Fishbein's local press reports on the new residents of Tel Aviv. In 1993, Tel Aviv's central bus station—the largest in the entire Middle East, the largest in the whole wide world, except in New Delhi—which had been under construction for ages, was finally all done. It devastated an already-run-down quarter. The older Jewish population, of Arab and Caucasus descent, had been evicted, or was migrating or dying out. Tin and wood shacks from the 1930s still survive in a small enclave on a hill, but the adjacent tiny cottages with their protected tenants now stand to be replaced by office blocks. Filipina migrant workers moved into the gloomy refurbished industrial projects and unglorified Bauhaus boxes that keep falling apart around the broken marketplace arches—what's left of the ghost of Palestine past. Eventually it became too eerie for the Filipinas, and they moved out. Now it's mostly Sudanese and Eritrean refugees. Palestinians keep passing through, their profiles hanging low, trying to avoid nasty encounters with border police patrols.

That's where my activism started, and it involved a choice. I chose migrant workers. Alienated by Israeli soldierdom, I chose those victims of state-enabled exploitation, living under a sword hanging by a precarious legal-status thread, so even so-called legal workers can be deported overnight. Later on my choice of activism became more and more diverse. The local green patch (where the homeless of all creeds and nations sleep, and used syringes go to die, not far from where I carpool every Friday to demonstrate in the West Bank) hosted our J14 social justice tent encampment, the summer before Occupy Wall Street began.

At first, when joining West Bank actions, I was still more apprehensive of those lurking, evil Palestinians who might be out to get me than I was of soldiers who posed a genuine threat to my well-being. But activism turned out to be a slippery slope. The more active I was, the more I knew about the market and state. The more I knew about the market and state, the more I felt alienated by the society I lived in. The more I felt alienated, the more I retreated from the life of mainstream gay Tel Aviv into that of the anarcho-activist scene.

◆

Across the river from the central bus station (that is, across the more or less imaginary Ayalon River) lies Kfar Shalem. Kfar Shalem (the Hebrewized namesake of the Palestinian village of Salame) was where Jewish Yemenite immigrants, who had been lodged in houses left behind by Palestinian refugees, were dispossessed and evicted when the state that had put them there decided, sixty years after the fact, that they had no right to their homes, and must make way for real estate entrepreneurs. Many of the people who used to go to West Bank demos were organizing actions with the tenants who were about to be thrown out—tenants who belonged to the very soldier nation that alienates activists so much.

Standing in solidarity with people who spoke my language, shared my citizenship, and served in my army felt stranger than standing in solidarity with Palestinians and migrant workers. When I encounter Palestinian nationalism or chauvinism, it's easy for me to set it aside by telling myself that my solidarity is with their place as victims of the Israeli occupation, and that I, an occupier, a participant in the violence that enables much of this nationalism and chauvinism, can't cast judgment. Criticizing from my position won't do any good; it will only reassert my position as the whiter man who knows better and pretends to speak from a higher moral ground. My place, then, is to express solidarity with their struggles on their terms, especially (but not only) where these struggles challenge nationalism and chauvinism, building the scaffolding for our common future struggles for a better life together beyond the occupation. But when it came to my Jewish Israeli compatriots in Kfar Shalem, I felt that their nationalist and conservative agenda was something I must reject, because it was the kind that I was dealing with daily. In Kfar Shalem, I was in solidarity with people who were close enough to alienate me.

I know that this analysis is flawed on so many levels. But this is how it felt. And in many ways, rationalizations and identity deconstruction notwithstanding, this is how it still so often feels. The ethnic repression and class gaps that separate me from many of the people of Kfar Shalem don't get me to withhold my privilege-enabled criticism as does the occupation gap between Palestinians and me. The way my education, income, and white man perks enable religious nationalism in Kfar Shalem doesn't seem to excuse the inhabitants' local vices as it does for Palestinians, or migrants, or refugees. The xenophobia and chauvinism that I see in Kfar Shalem are so much closer to those that I grew up with, to those in whose terms I still all too often think, to those that strike so close to home, that I can't hold them at bay.

When radical leftists in Israel engage in solidarity with Israeli Jews, we often have this fantasy of finding a working-class hero, preferably a woman, who despite not having had the kind of education and socialization that taught us to see Israel/Palestine as we do, would nevertheless intuitively come up with our hard-earned political views. She would be proud of her heritage as Mizrahi (a Jew of Arab descent), she would be an uncompromising feminist, she would see Zionism as a movement of white elitist colonial dispossession, and yet she would be rooted in her community, leading it to stand up and resist. But this working-class hero is hardly ever there. If she's there, she's usually as alienated from the community that she's supposed to lead as I am from my own middle-class milieu, the Zionists of Ashkenaz. And then we're quick to pick up on her little racisms, and classisms, and conservatisms, and she falls from grace. Her little faults are easy to pick up on; she's close enough to us for us to see in her what we work so hard to pretend we've overcome ourselves.

◆

Which sends me back to that alienating mirror: middle-class Ashkenazis (or those who've become so entrenched in the Israeli middle class that they no longer have a marked ethnicity, and sometimes project this "feat" onto others, falsely claiming that Jewish ethnic divisions are no longer a barrier in Israel). After the failure of the Oslo process, the radical Left abandoned whatever little faith it had in the shattered Zionist Left. Zionist leftists came to be seen as indistinguishable from the Zionist Center-Right. And when finally, in 2010, some Zionist leftists resurfaced around the movement Solidarity Sheikh Jarrah, the encounter didn't work.

Solidarity Sheikh Jarrah was a movement reacting to settlers taking over Palestinian homes in East Jerusalem. Its rhetoric marked 1967 as the fault line. Its implicit view was that Zionist colonialism was justified up until 1967— that it was the encroachment on Palestinian property on the other side of the 1949 armistice line (the effective border until the 1967 war) that constituted the primordial Israeli sin. This view accompanies that of a two-state vision and no right of return for Palestinian refugees. It's a position that the Ashkenazi middle class often finds easy to endorse. It doesn't mark the historic state building by this class as wrong; it does not recognize its exploitation and oppression of Mizrahi Jews and Palestinians as akin in any way; and it does not require that this class pay a price. It's strictly the right-wing settlers who are at fault and must therefore give up their homes, while economic colonization by the middle class would no doubt continue in the form of "bilateral economic cooperation" after a Palestinian state is formed.

Solidarity Sheikh Jarrah was an opportunity to reach out to the Zionist Left. But few in the radical Left managed to stick in for a long-term effort. What many of us saw in Sheikh Jarrah was the soldier mentality, the so-called shooting-and-crying syndrome: instigating violence and then lamenting its impact on our own tender souls. The movement had a rather impressive peak and some solid achievements on the ground, but now it's dwindling as it searches for a path. Many of the Zionists didn't stick around. Us radicals observe, conduct postmortems over tactics, and keep telling ourselves how right we've all been all along.

◆

Then came the J14 movement. It started as a protest against rent in Tel Aviv and exploded immediately into a social justice movement. Hundreds of tents in the main Tel Aviv camp, dozens of other tent camps all over Israel, and hundreds of thousands marching together in what may have been Israel's largest demonstrations ever.

But what radical leftists saw there was the popular culture of music festivals and postarmy round-the-world trips of young people clearing their heads in that sweet limbo between oppressing Palestinians and harnessing themselves to the capitalist machine that would turn them into fodder for corporate jobs. Unity was the name of the game. The popular cry was "revolution," but demanding that the government resign was considered unnecessarily divisive (and indeed, since all Israeli governments, left and right alike, oppressed Palestinians and implemented an elite-friendly economic policy, changing the government would probably be meaningless). The protest was supposed to unite the Left and Right, so discussing the occupation was taboo. The movement wanted unity over anything else—a mythical Israeli solidarity that's supposed to have existed in the early days of yore.

Some radical leftists chose to join the Palestinian protest camp in Jaffa, the Palestinian-citizen-of-Israel backyard of Tel Aviv, rather than face the Israeli ex-soldier colony in the center of the city. Some brought Jaffa to central Tel Aviv as the "1948 tent," which tried to convey the Palestinian story to the Jewish protesters. Some opted to set up camp next to the central bus station, forming a small tent encampment housing local Israeli Jews together with street dweller refugees and drug addicts. I felt more comfortable there than in central Tel Aviv. The central bus station tent camp was violent, messy, and dysfunctional, yet it allowed me to be in solidarity with "others" rather than face my "own" community of peers. It was extremely hard to communicate with people in our camp, but I had language, culture, and class barriers to blame. In central Tel Aviv the only barrier would be that of alienation, which is, apparently, a barrier that is far harder for me to cross.

I love Tel Aviv. Unlike most activists around me, I can't see myself living anywhere else. But I can't face Tel Aviv. I play along in mainstream Tel Aviv, enjoying my friends, the culture, the weather, and the uncannily beautiful, crumbling (and all the more beautiful for crumbling) architecture. But for my activism I go to the central bus station. I'd rather separate my activism from my daily city life. I act in solidarity with people whose plight has to do with my privilege. Since I am part of their problem, it's pointless for me to patronize them over how their communities go wrong; my role is to work in solidarity when they fight to make things better. With those who share my privileges though not my politics, with those whose wrongs are so densely interlinked with mine, I feel that I don't have enough of a common language to talk about what's wrong.

◆

Recently, I changed my function at the worker rights nongovernmental organization where I used to do advocacy on behalf of migrant workers. I now give out labor rights information to disadvantaged Israeli citizen workers. Perhaps it's yet another way of not talking to my own community about the occupation. But then again, perhaps something starts to give.

—Roy Wagner

Running with Wolves

narchists Against the Wall's biggest success is our ability to honestly look at our Jewish privilege (whether
we're Jewish or not) within Israel's system of military
occupation and apartheid. Taking this responsibility—
owning up to our privileged position within the system of
apartheid and acting on that premise as the day-to-day situations demand—enables us to create political bonds with
each other. Yet these bonds, which form the group within
which we act together, often remain merely in the political realm and steer away from the personal. They are not
friendships (though that sometimes occurs), they do not
accommodate anything of the emotional sort, and to me
that may just be the problem.

Over the years of my activism with AAtW, it has
become clearer to me that there's a strong tradition of a
"self-sufficient lone wolf" in the group: the activist who
only works within the context of a team or group for lack
of functional resources. This tendency is rooted in the notion that we have to "professionalize" our relationships
with each other within the group, know as little as possible

about each other, and not dwell on anything other than what is needed for political analysis.

On the face of it, this is a "pragmatic" approach that allows us to be efficient and goal oriented. However, I believe that this approach not only erodes our ability to function as individuals within a group and as a group but also is the opposite of the anarchist vision that many of us hold.

When I took my first ride with AAtW to Bil'in, I didn't think about socializing. I was thinking, "I must bear witness to the oppression of the Palestinian people." As fate would have it, I met some extraordinarily nice people with the added value of anarchist politics. I would come to love and care for these people, and we would share life-threatening, life-altering, intellectually challenging, and plain-old-emotional moments. I write this piece because I believe there's a direct connection between community and the ability to survive as an action group. I write it so other action groups and the individuals they are made of won't erode themselves as a result of lack of intersolidarity, which in my view is key to self-preservation and—as such—our survival.

I Didn't Come Here to Make Friends

For the four years in which I've been and continue to be an active participant in AAtW, the issue of the "individualists" in our group has been a popular topic of speculation and theorizing. Everything from posttrauma, misanthropy, Asperger's syndrome, shyness, social awkwardness, and good old-fashioned assholism has been considered. I write my final analysis in this article: machoism.

Since I define feminism as a prism from which we analyze women's struggle, I deduce that *not* being feminist isn't anarchist. And this point—I constantly discover—is a perpetual thorn in the side of anarchist (and wider leftist) communities worldwide.

Typically, we find that our self-sufficient lone wolves shy away from talking about "emotional issues" (that is, "intergroup politics") inside the group, and that the excuse is always the same: there's always a fire to put out first.

Dissent with this deeply rooted group dynamic—an insistence on prioritizing emotional issues/intergroup politics—is met with immediate marginalization: presence at meetings dwindles, AAtW members are made to feel coerced, and discussions are hurried along, because the process is "taking energy from the group." Unfortunately this is textbook sexist behavior of the more subtle kind, which is—more often than not—led by heterosexual, white/Ashkenazi males, who are in fact a minority within the group.

That said, macho behavior that enshrines the "silent, fearless activist who gets gassed and shot and comes back smiling and limping next week for more" is practiced across the gender board within the group. Sometimes this is the only way to deal with reoccurring trauma, lacking any other supportive outlets, and sometimes it is ingrained, taught "male behavior" that's been brought from wherever each of us grew up (Israeli society at large). Both bad education and lack of support intertwine into a circular pattern of macho, hero worship culture, which then strips us of our ability to create a support system from which we can enter the literal war zones in which we act.

"What Community"?

Just these dynamics will eventually destroy the most committed of action groups. And while a semblance of a group exists, my feeling is that there's not so much a group but instead a number of people who do the same thing, at the same time, in the same place every week. And while I often say this outright, those who don't give it any thought inadvertently give voice to this feeling in the most critical of circumstances.

As within any group of people who come together from different backgrounds, conflicts of class frequently occur. Unfortunately, AAtW, which excels at analyzing global matters through an anarchist prism, hasn't taken its anarchism to that next level of analyzing interpersonal relationships through that same prism.

It appears an outlook has taken root, according to which the fact that we come from the Jewish side of apartheid means that we automatically live a life of excess. In reality, though, we come from all walks of life, ethnicities, socioeconomic backgrounds, genders, and identities. This demands a nuanced position as we face the question of acknowledging our own oppressions. And while the existence of a diversity of identities as well as the intersectionality of oppressions and privilege are well understood in theory,

when these identities are asserted, we find that we are progressive on nothing but Palestine.

As I've stated before, intergroup politics are regard-
ed as emotional issues that take energy from the group.
So how do we solve the problem of a member who's been
constantly accused of sexual violence? Or the problem of
a member who acts irresponsibly in the field, endangering
the lives and safety of others? Or the problem of someone
who "I just don't like," and after years of dedicated work
finds themselves excluded from action? Or the most common problem: a member who's suffering from posttraumatic stress?

Predictably, we turn our heads to "more pressing issues." And when the word "community" is brought up, we
wash our hands of responsibility with the simple and cynical query, "What community?"

This question exemplifies my aforementioned sense
that there is, in fact, no group. Yet these feelings do not
negate the fact that a community exists by default: we're a
small number of people who have been collaborating for
more than seven years, and suffering extreme experiences
together (or at least while in each other's presence). And
so we're left with two options: being a shitty community
whose members continuously punish each other (often by
the simple nonaction of withholding common courtesies);
or being a community that makes a consistent, continuous effort to create a safe space for each other (a novel idea,
I know . . .), and allows its members to be vulnerable and
honest, and care for each other.

The Walls Must Fall

It is rare that we, as a group, discuss power dynamics within AAtW. It's even rarer that we document such conversations. In his book *Anarchy Alive!* Uri Gordon points to the inadvertent manner in which dynamics of domination come into being, often "reproduced through performative disciplinary acts in which protagonists may not even be conscious of their roles." In order to break these behavioral cycles, all that's required is taking responsibility, choosing a target, and taking action (yet another novel idea . . .). Since stopping the macho defense mechanism that this group has collectively adopted as a reaction to trauma operates on a plane that group dynamics prohibit us from accessing, it seems to me that the best place to start is self-education.

While we're all versed in the minutest of laws concerning closed military areas near a specific checkpoint, not enough heterosexual male anarchists have taken the time to read about sexism as oppressive social/legal/military systems that discriminate against women and queers. Somehow the analysis connecting the occupation of land with the occupation of the female (body and identity) has completely eluded them. Its importance is seen as secondary, if it is acknowledged at all. Even less attention is paid to Mizrahi or Russian-speaking identity, or to those connected to age, disability, or spirituality.

Since a lack of feminist education (basic statistics about rape, for example) is so prevalent, I've had to find ways of communicating the message and creating translation for my strange feminist tongue. I find it instructive to use the Palestinian prism of analysis in order to point out the workings of sexism within the group by, for example, equating a sexual predator to a right-wing politician like Avigdor Lieberman or those who enable gender violence (by not wanting to take energy from the group) to the Zionists in Peace Now, or linking my reaction to such violence to the boycott, divestment, and sanctions campaign. This, in turn, has allowed me to strengthen the old feminist assertion that "the personal is political," and that speaking of our emotions/interpersonal politics is just as anarchistic and worthy as planning the next direct action.

Interestingly, the Palestinian prism has protected me from the typical "troublemaker," "divisive," and "busybody" labels that could have erupted under such explosive circumstances. At the same time, connecting the struggles did a lot for many of us in dismantling the macho stereotypes and clichés that prevent us from doing this essential community-building work.

That said, our own inner community work has just begun, and it's hard to tell whether the lack of interest is because of years of disappointment or a commitment to anarcho-individualism. I put my money on the former and commit myself to an anarcha-feminist plan of action.

To Exist Is to Resist!

In Israel, a cunning word has snuck into the Hebrew language, *hamatzáv*, which translates as "the situation." The term refers to that pesky problem of Palestinians. Though it's much less blatantly racist than "the Jewish problem," for example, its insidious effect is in its most literal definition. A situation is a given fact, which is tangible and unchangeable. This phrase enables a structure of thinking in which "the situation" is a stagnant reality, and deflates action before it even comes to mind. Even worse, it completely diminishes the ability to discern that, in fact, the situation here, as anywhere, is in constant flux.

Even though "the situation" is an Israeli concoction, it describes quite precisely the general situation of despair, which our violent world instills in people. Since this world doesn't pause on our arrival to allow us to catch up, it's incumbent on us to hit the ground running in order to survive. This may sound like a kind of biodeterminist rationale for a depressing worldview, but to me, anarchism doesn't exist if constant responsibility and accountability aren't practiced toward one another. On the one hand, that means that anarchism is necessarily an ideal notion that can never be attained. On the other hand, anarchism means that even though practice will never make perfect, we continue to try. And that, to me, is a positive way to spend one's time on this planet.

Four years ago I arrived in the anarchist world. I wasn't there when it was created, and I inherited all its blessings and catastrophes. In time I would come to realize that—for lack of blessings—a lot of what we do as activists is to turn catastrophe into opportunity. On the solidarity-with-Palestinians front, we document the army's violence, so we can show the world what happens here. On the intergroup-politics front, I've found that the constant employment of an anarchist analysis of the balance of power is indispensable. Putting things squarely on the table (or "calling out" . . . more novel ideas!) when they go awry, allows us to revisit and redefine what is and isn't acceptable in the group. This in turn reshapes our language, which in turn reshapes our reality, and so on.

My experience with AAtW strengthens my understanding that destructive group dynamics, rooted in wider societal norms of oppression, are alive and well inside anarchist communities. More often than not, I find that we replicate the banalities of evil that we so fervently struggle against. I believe that if we simply care for one another and do not condemn the materialization of emotional bonds as a hindrance to our political goals, we might achieve some glimpse of this constantly in flux anarchist ideal. It may be a simplistic thesis pertaining to a complex dynamic, but I truly believe we must stop looking at accountability as a chore or a price we pay. A community based on constant introspection *is* an anarchist community. Accountability is our reward.

Indeed, we can't always exemplify accountability in practice. Weaker members will always need an alternative way to level the playing field with the stronger members, and more often than not, the only way to do this is through a subversive act. That said, the analysis of imbalances of power already maps the justification for this act. Thus, accountability is established de facto both for the privileged and underprivileged member, and it's outlined by the underprivileged. Engaging in analysis of oppression as it happens is that critical first step toward taking responsibility for ourselves, our oppression, and our community.

I find that as long as we continue asserting our identities, keep defining and redefining the analysis of imbalance of power and privilege, make it present and organize against it within the community, creating solidarity with each other, we will reemerge from any catastrophe empowered and better acquainted, and as a result, spaces open up—just enough for us to be able to start scratching the surface of our collective trauma.

—Tali Shapiro

Here, Murderers Are Heroes

On Tuesday evening, July 27, 2008, a few of us gathered at the Vegan Community House for a meeting. Shortly before the meeting was scheduled to begin, we received the news: the army had murdered a child in Ni'ilin. Minutes later, five of us quickly headed out to the village. When we got there, hundreds of people were in the streets, rioting out of sheer fury over the death of their neighbor, friend, brother, and son. The army, too, was rioting. It had invaded the village, with its armored jeeps and M16-toting soldiers. About an hour earlier, ten-year-old Ahmed Musa along with a small group of kids and teenagers had approached the wall's construction site and were messing with the razor wire installed around it by the army. A military jeep approached them, shooting rubber bullets. The kids ran away, but in his escape, Ahmed Musa lost his sandal. When he returned to pick it up, a soldier got out of the jeep and shot a single live bullet into the little boy's forehead, killing him on the spot. The others, including his own brother, carried his lifeless body back to the village, leaving a thick trail of blood through the ancient olive groves. From there he was transferred to the hospital in Ramallah, where shortly after, his body was sent to the morgue.

Faced with the despair and deep sadness that slowly started accompanying the initial rage, the five of us headed toward Ramallah as the riots quieted down, hoping for something—confirmation of the unbelievable maybe, or perhaps simply to offer the family our support. Yet the family was already gone when we arrived. For a reason I cannot clearly remember, we were taken to the morgue by one of the doctors, where Ahmed's tiny body lay inanimate.

The sight hit me with shock. I had never seen a dead body before, let alone that of a child. I didn't know how to react or what to say. Anger, frustration, and pain flooded my body. Though the army's cruelty and violence are nothing new, I could not understand how a ten-year-old could have ever been perceived as a threat to a soldier.

The following day, at the funeral, thousands of people from all over the West Bank came to show their solidarity and share their pain with Ahmed Musa's family. We were there too, lost for words.

In the evening, after the funeral, rage took over the streets of Ni'ilin once again, and clashes erupted as the army invaded the village. Yousef Amirah, seventeen years old, was in a yard close to the clashes, observing. An armored jeep pulled up in the street in front of him, and a soldier shot three rounds of rubber-coated bullets from inside the jeep through the firing loophole. Two bullets ended up lodged inside Yousef's skull. Minutes later, he was pronounced clinically dead at the Ramallah hospital, and died of his injuries a few days after.

The shock was once again terrible. Two murdered kids in two days. When we returned from the village, we joined others in an impromptu demonstration in front of the home of the minister of defense, Ehud Barak. Despite our rage, surrounded by dozens of cops, all we could do was block one of Tel Aviv's main roads for a short time and shout slogans while we held the murdered children's pictures in our hands.

Though I stood there and shouted along with others, my rage was not only directed at Barak. Barak is indeed responsible for the murder of Ahmed and Yousef, and countless others before them, but he and the government he represents are certainly not the only ones. To me, Israeli citizens are the ones to point the finger at; they are the ones who elected these politicians, and they are the ones who wholeheartedly support the government as it commits murder and wages war. Israeli citizens are the ones who do not revolt against racism, apartheid, and ethnic cleansing. In fact, all these are no more than a crystallization of Israeli public opinion.

Israeli children are brainwashed, from birth, to believe that Israel must be a Jewish state, Palestinians are the enemy, and military service is a sacred duty—no matter the cost, no matter who is hurt. But despite this powerful indoctrination, we are all responsible for our actions. Though conscription is compulsory, decent people can always make a decent choice. Faced with such widespread Israeli compliance with the crimes of our government, I cannot escape the conclusion that we are all accomplices through our silence, through the lack of deed.

From Zionism to Anarchy

I was not born in Israel, nor was I born an anarchist. I immigrated to Israel from Canada in 2001. I was a Zionist and believed my place in the world was in Israel, the only haven for Jews. In 2006, a friend who often attended demonstrations in the West Bank showed me the other side of my reality. It took me a full year to grasp the essence of the occupation and rid myself of the brainwash I never knew I had undergone.

One Friday in May 2007, I arrived at the village of Bil'in for the first time, where Israel's wall was being built on villagers' land. There, for the first time, all the pieces came together—I could see, with my own eyes, Israeli apartheid. From then on, demonstrations became a weekly thing, the forming of a habit.

Before I knew it, I started going to AAtW meetings and demonstrations, becoming more heavily involved. Soon enough I was organizing the transportation for our Friday expeditions. Being part of those who decide, those who do, was an empowering experience. I met people from different backgrounds, ages, shapes, and colors, all different, yet united by the same cause. We are all driven by the wish to fight the occupation and apartheid. We hardly ever bother with promoting our various grand-scheme-of-things ideas. Once the occupation is behind us, we will have the luxury to discuss our diverse opinions.

I am perfectly aware that our actions alone will not end Israeli apartheid. It will take much more than that. But I believe (or want to believe) that we disrupt Israel along with its notion of "peace and quiet." I want to believe that when we march down the streets of Tel Aviv with banners calling for an end to the war, bystanders are forced to think. Perhaps our mere presence in the streets, our actions, will bring the consequences of the occupation to their backyard—and not some twenty kilometers away. Even those who call us traitors or self-hating Jews are in fact reacting to the occupation. To an extent I derive some comfort from such comments, since they show we are forcing people to be aware that there is an occupation and that Palestinians do exist.

The massacre in Gaza, in which more than thirteen hundred people were killed, was for us the ultimate proof that Israel is engaged in ethnic cleansing. Again, though I am perfectly aware of the government's capability to commit such crimes—even to feel comfortable while doing so—something about how this "war" was conducted felt revolting in new, unfamiliar ways. Even more appalling was the fact that 80 percent of the Israeli public supported the slaughter.

During those days, the sense of frustration and hopelessness overwhelmed us all. We organized demonstrations daily, and joined other demonstrations in Palestinian villages and cities, inside Israel and in the West Bank, but there was nothing we could do to stop the wheels of that runaway train—Israeli fascism.

There was something else, too, apart from the incomprehensible dimensions of the catastrophe in Gaza. In the West Bank, we have gotten used to things being accessible. When, for instance, a murder occurs somewhere in the

West Bank, we are able to get there, physically; the apartheid segregation is not total. The Gaza strip, however, is impenetrable for us.

This time, we could only demonstrate, shout slogans, and read the news. There was a feeling of being imprisoned within Israel's borders. Though utterly different, I could suddenly understand, personally, what it meant to have my movement restricted.

But perhaps we did manage to disrupt something, because the police and Israeli secret service targeted Palestinians living in Israel, and to a lesser degree, activists in AAtW. Many were arrested and then interrogated for hours without any reason other than intimidation. In one of the court hearings, a prosecutor actually said that our actions "damage the morale of Israeli soldiers"—this, from the so-called only democracy in the Middle East.

Personally, I do not think I will see the end of the occupation in my lifetime—I am thirty years old. Most Israelis do not care about Palestinians, or for that matter, even about crimes against humanity committed against them. Palestinians are far too remote to be present in the pains and minds of most Israelis. Who needs to feel the occupation while sitting in a coffee shop or eating hummus in Jaffa? Israel exists in a bubble. When I see the path of the wall, I ask myself, Who is locking who in? Israel can only look toward the sea on its West, as it has locked shut all doors to the Middle East.

Though I believe that our work within Israel is crucial, I am also aware of the fact that our voice is faint and hardly heard. The occupation and Israeli apartheid can only come to an end if such an end is forced on them, mainly through boycotts, sanctions, and other forms of international pressure. As the status quo continues, boycott—economic, academic, and cultural—is the only effective way to pressure Israel. But I have no illusions; it seems as if the world has not yet seen enough Palestinian blood. The road ahead of us is still long.

Until then, the struggle continues.

—Sarah Assouline

Emotional First Aid

One of the amazing things about activists is that we often deliberately expose ourselves to brutality when we believe it necessary.[1] But being exposed to violence without being prepared, having support or processing what happened afterward can have a harmful effect on our mental and physical health. Radical activists in Israel/Palestine run from one action to the next. It feels like everything is urgent. We don't always prepare for actions—sit down beforehand and discuss possible scenarios, and talk about what we need or how we feel. Although we designate specific people to be in charge of arrests, first aid, or media, we don't have a trauma-support person. Trauma is still perceived as an after-the-fact issue, if at all. In a place with such intense activism, it's easy to feel there's no time to deal with activist trauma, though awareness is rising.

In 2006, inspired by groups that organized in Europe against the G8, a small group of us in Tel Aviv formed the "T-Team," an activist trauma team. In our training, we learned about trauma support and worked from our own experiences, to relate to what others were going through. We began offering support in the form of workshops and

one-on-one sessions, and distributing written materials. We
made ourselves available to organizations we ourselves were
a part of, such as AAtW. In each AAtW weekly email, we
included a few words about activist trauma and our contact
information. Though the T-Team is no longer active, these
issues are becoming more acceptable to talk about.

This contribution discusses issues of trauma and burnout among activists who are repeatedly exposed to intense
violence, through participation in actions against the occupation. It includes excerpts from interviews with fellow
activists, and draws on books and zines on the subject.

Struggle and Stress: Activist Trauma

Trauma refers to a wound of the soul, mind, or emotional
core, and is created when a person stands helpless against
an external threat without sufficient resources to deal with
it. The stability in the person's internal and external world
is disrupted, control is taken away, and instead of order
and safety, there is a feeling that things are arbitrary; they
can then feel in a state of constant expectation of the next
threat or catastrophe.[2]

> I remember at my first protests against the wall
> in Bil'in . . . the most violent thing that I did was
> to yell a little, and suddenly my legs were covered
> in bruises, just covered! And I thought to myself,
> "Whoa, hold on a second, the people around me,
> myself included, never covered our faces, there was

no violent breakout to trigger this" . . . I think that's
what went through me, that . . . "Wait, what's going
on here"?[3]

We are exposed to trauma in many situations, including harassment by police or military, or getting beat up or
arrested. Seeing an event take place from the sidelines (such
as witnessing night raids or watching someone else get
hurt) can also be traumatic, even though we don't tend to
think of it that way.[4]

Facing a threat can take seconds, hours, days, or
more—until we get to a safe place. During the time of
the threat, it's hard to preserve a sense of control. There
are instinctual responses to trauma, like freezing in place,
running to somewhere safe, or fighting. It is important to
remember these are instincts; if we see them as choices, we
might feel guilt about how we behaved.

In Beit Liqia there was a crazy demo; the army was
shooting all over the place. A bunch of kids started
to kick and pass around the tear gas canisters that
were shot at them as if they were playing soccer,
only among whistling bullets. Their mothers stood
on the hill and started crying and screaming for
them to come back. I tried to calm down the mothers, even though I don't speak Arabic. I started crying too. Then the soldiers just lost it, and everyone
started running back to the village for protection.
As we ran, we saw there were snipers on the roof-
tops at the entrance. It felt like, "OK, soldiers are

running after us, and other soldiers are waiting for us there." We just ran. Some people were shot on the way. Some were injured and fell down. There was no processing of that experience. We were all just starting out in the struggle. We didn't know what to expect or how to prepare.

It's sometimes hard to recognize that we feel scared or weak during an action; all systems are focused on surviving. In this state, it's critical to feel support and connection to others.

During actions I didn't feel helpless. We didn't really talk about affinity groups, and when people did, they usually didn't work. But I knew very well to choose who I went with, and in the heat of things I trusted their judgment and they trusted mine. I felt that closeness, that trust, others looking out for me, and I for them. It's hard to tell how much danger I was in, but physically I wasn't harmed as bad as I could have been. Maybe it's just luck.

The aftermath of trauma can bring about a number of symptoms referred to as *posttraumatic stress* (PTS).[5] PTS is a normal response to abnormal circumstances, an effort made by a person who experienced trauma to go back to their regular life. The brain wants to go back to the traumatic event to understand what happened.[6] At the same time, it is too difficult to do that, so the body doesn't allow it to happen directly. This is a mechanism originally meant to protect us, but over a long period of exposure to trauma, it can become harmful.

PTS symptoms include *disassociation*—a feeling of not being fully in the present, or not being able to remember what happened, yet feeling constantly haunted by it; *avoidance*—avoiding thoughts, emotions, or conversations about the trauma, which may result in distancing oneself from people or places associated with the event; *physical problems* such as muscle pains, headaches, and breathing problems; *flashbacks*—seeing pieces of the traumatic event in short snippets during the day or night; *triggers*—seeing, smelling, tasting, hearing, or experiencing something that is reminiscent of the trauma can make us feel as if we are suddenly transported right back to the event; *hypervigilance*—not being able to calm down, having trouble falling asleep or waking up, feeling anxious, or seeing danger everywhere.

> There are situations I was in that even the thought of them scares me. And I didn't do much with this fear; it would dissipate at some point in all the action. And to think how did this affect me later? Emotionally, I understood it when I'd see the shadow of a bird flying overhead and think it's a stun grenade.

It's important to remember that these symptoms are warning signs. It doesn't mean you're going crazy, but it's essential not to ignore such symptoms as other problems associated with PTS may develop. While experiencing these symptoms, it is crucial that we have support.

Processing trauma may happen informally, on the ride home from an action, or with a friend or partner. If that person is not supportive, PTS can worsen. Although we may expect those who share our political views to be most supportive, it's not always the case.

> I would ride home with other activists, people who were really engaged in this struggle. Especially in the relationship with my ex-partner. . . . The way she sees it, it's the Palestinians who are suffering, and we . . . we can be an instrument, we do serve some purpose, but our suffering doesn't matter in this situation, there is no room for it . . . it isn't legitimate. When we got back from protests bruised, we sometimes took pictures so there would be some kind of proof, in case of a trial. When we talked about it, she said it's really machoistic, like, "Look at me, I got hurt here and here." So I started feeling like, "Oh well, people were at this protest and got beaten up, what's the big deal?"

What about Burnout?

> At some point, I can't remember what year, the subject of trauma came down heavily on the anarchist community. . . . Many people burned out and left. . . . You looked left and right, and you didn't recognize anyone [at the demonstration] that was there one year earlier.

Experiencing trauma over time can make us "burn out"—feel exhausted on the inside, lose our spark, feel depleted, frustrated, or stop coming to actions altogether. It is a process that can take days, weeks, or years. Some people get over burnout by themselves, and others may need outside help.

Burnout is different from tiredness. There is "good" or healthy tiredness, and then there is chronic exhaustion.[7] It can also influence us at home and in our relationships, and lead to depression. Because of the urgency of our activism, we might not stop to take care of ourselves, continue "running on empty," feel desensitized to violence, and therefore misjudge what is safe and what is dangerous.

> I never stopped going to demos. There was a time when I went very often, but when I took breaks and returned, it seemed like one of the most absurd situations that one could consciously put oneself in. It was crazy, in the sense of having reality slap you in the face. I saw brutal stuff. Eventually I just convinced myself that this is the way things are. I would get back in time to walk my dog, knowing fifteen minutes away from my home is this other reality. I remember the huge gap between the reality I witnessed, and the calm, carefree life that is a short distance away. At first it even made me a bit angry and frustrated . . . kind of helpless. But mostly I just felt tired.

Symptoms associated with burnout include a negative self-image; growing negative feelings toward the source of burnout and others who are involved with that source; constantly wishing events were canceled; feeling impatient; feeling overloaded and meaningless at the same time; becoming cold, rude, or distant from others who might witness our breakage, and sometimes even taking out anger and frustration on other activists (which is, of course, completely contradictory to our work).

> There is trauma, that's true. We're dealing with really difficult stuff. There are also different kinds of people—I don't think there's anyone who doesn't get traumatized. But some people really suppress it well and they're fine with it, and with others it erupts later on . . . and it comes out in things that have nothing to do with their trauma, which I think happened to me a little too. So how do you deal? People who repress it, how are they to help the ones who are completely broken from it? They think that they are fine and they won't find a common language with the ones hurting, and then you're left with a big group of people who cannot support one another.

Reclaiming Our Health

Although each of us experiences them individually, activist trauma and burnout are collective issues. They influence how we interact with the world, where we feel able to go, and what we feel able to do. To effectively deal with them, and continue to be active in the struggle against the occupation, we need to take care of ourselves.

Recognizing What's Going On

When it comes to trauma, what we don't know *can* hurt us. Not knowing we are traumatized doesn't prevent us from having problems that are caused by it.[8] We can start by talking to each other as well as accessing information about these issues online and through printed materials. Groups like Activist Trauma Team (http://www.activist-trauma. net) already have plenty of material available. Activist pattrice jones also wrote an excellent book titled *Aftershock!* We don't have to become experts on trauma, but we should know how to respond to each other in a healthy way. It'll help us be more aware during actions.

> Today I go to fewer demos than I used to. I recognize when I feel weak—I usually have stomachaches even before I get there—and during an action, especially around tear gas, I get nauseous and dizzy. In that situation I run to find the closest house and go in.

Trauma doesn't just come up in conversation, because in many cultures it has a social stigma of weakness. We've got to remember our boundaries, go with the people we feel safe with, and make time for processing our experiences after an action, both in the group and on our own. What does

this mean? It can start with a quick group check-in immediately after, before everyone splits; talking to someone we
trust when we get home; getting some food together, and
talking about what worked fantastically and what didn't.

> Today there is more space for processing. There is
> an informal social ritual—that after the Friday dem-
> onstrations we all go to the same hummus place to
> eat and talk about what happened. We try to make
> sure that new people come along.

Taking Care of Ourselves

If exposure to violence is taking a heavy toll, it may be
necessary to ask for help, and rest and monitor one's physical health. We can use creative outlets to deal with emotions like anger, guilt, or frustration. Different kinds of art
can help preserve a sense of control during actions, be a tool
for processing or just a healthy outlet for what we feel.

> When I was in Hebron, there were all of these
> tough Jewish and Palestinian types, and we sat
> there and there was just nothing to do, so I drew a
> little. . . . Another time I drew the settlers throw-
> ing rocks and burning the Palestinians' laundry. I
> recorded this on video. . . . Sometimes reality here
> is just psychotic. Through the years I wrote songs
> and poems. . . . I even made a comedy about my
> life once.

I remember when I first got to Beit Surik, I thought to make bracelets out of a cut wire fence. I did it at the beginning until the kids stole my pliers.

Outside help, like different kinds of therapy, can be helpful. *Psychoactive: Mental Health Professionals for Human Rights* (http://www.psychoactive.org.il) offers therapy and other resources for activists in Israel/Palestine. We can also draw strength from small achievements and times when actions did make a difference.

In the territories I feel success when resistance works—like when the army tries to enter a village and people are able to block them until they leave. It makes me feel connected, a power created by mutual organizing. It provides an optimistic basis to think that things could be different.

Supporting Each Other

A lot of the time support is expressed very technically—as in a place to rest, food, and bail. When people get arrested and there's someone there to accompany them when they get released, that there's always someone there to sign your bail, someone who gets you food when you're arrested . . . things that are really small, but tell you that you're not alone.

Alongside physical support *during* an action, there's a lot we can do on a regular basis to help each other. We live in a crazy reality here. Mainstream society doesn't offer support for the causes we fight for. So we have to find the people and places that make us feel safe, loved, and free to talk openly; it's key for preventing and healing from trauma.

> I'd be at Sheikh Jarrah, I'll get shoved and roughed up, and you can't go here and there, and more houses are taken over and it's really awful. And still I come home to dinner with my girlfriend, and my energy rises again. It isn't that I forget that people live there in tents and such, but that I can take in something good.

In activist circles, it often feels like taking care of ourselves is selfish, when there is always an urgent action to deal with. But taking care of ourselves is also a social action—to preserve our strength and remain active in a place where injustices are so profound. The healthier we are, the more we can do, the more we can offer support and the more our work is, ultimately, sustainable. Taking steps to deal with these issues is vital to our health as individuals as well as for ongoing work as a group.

—Iris Arieli

Means of Communication

Any anarchist watching Eran Torbiner's 2005 documentary *Matzpen: Anti-Zionist Israelis* would find it easy to identify with those who were on Israel's political margins forty years ago. The idea of establishing a Palestinian state, which placed the members of Matzpen beyond the pale, is today a consensual position in Israeli politics. And this journey that ideas make, from the hold of a minority group to the heart of the majority, depends to a great extent on the media that feeds the latter. These are the media that define the consensus, and therefore also those responsible for changing it. This is the reason for my insistence on continuing my affair with Israeli media. As both an activist and a journalist I recognize the media's ability to distribute knowledge, and believe in the ability of knowledge to create change.

As activists against the occupation, most of our information on the apartheid wall was gathered firsthand in the occupied territories. In the first months of the wall's construction, at the end of 2002, the Israeli media showed little interest in what appeared to be yet another uprooting of olive trees. An official map of the route of the barrier had not yet been published, and the newspaper desks received mainly photos of bulldozers telling an apparently old story. Except for a handful of reports by *Ha'aretz* journalists Amira Hass and Gideon Levy on the human tragedies taking place, and critical articles by B. Michael and Meron Rapoport in *Yedi'ot Aharonot*, the Israeli media was disinterested in Prime Minister Sharon's new construction project—the largest in Israel's history.

A new grouping called the Coalition against the Fence, whose goal was to present the Israeli public with critical information about the fence, had difficulty breaking through the veil of ignorance that accompanied the construction during the first year. If the wall was mentioned at all in Israeli media, it was in order to ask why it wasn't being built more quickly.

For Israeli objectors to the fence, the meaningful "coming-out" party took place in November 2003, at a demonstration in front of the Tel Aviv Cinematheque, on the anniversary of the fall of the Berlin wall (designated as an international day of resistance to the wall in Palestine). Despite disappointing coverage, the fact that opposition to the barrier exists began to percolate into Israeli public opinion. A large demonstration at A-Ram north of Jerusalem in December marked another budge.

In March, we, who for the most part do not feed off media self-defined as "Zionist," had already joined in activities against the wall in the village of Mas'ha (95 percent of whose lands are now on its "Israeli" side), and along with the residents, had created an information center. Following the activities in Mas'ha, we decided to join international activists in direct actions to cut and break through the fence as well as initiate such actions ourselves with Palestinian partners. In an action to cut the fence in the village of Zububa in November, we hadn't really decided whether to call ourselves Jews Against Ghettos or Anarchists Against the Wall. On Friday, December 23, we returned to Mas'ha in order to break open the gate in the fence that remained locked. An Israeli soldier shot at Gil Na'amati, who a few weeks earlier had held a weapon himself and worn the same uniform. The media sniffed drama and decided for us: "Anarchists Against the Wall." A new brand was born.

That Friday I came back from the action at Mas'ha exhausted and shaken. Still unable to digest the meaning of the events, I went to the pub with a few friends. That night I didn't sleep in my own house, and images of Gil wallowing in a pool of his own blood kept me awake. On Saturday morning I accessed my voicemail. Fifteen journalists had been looking for me. From that moment, a weeklong frenzy began. On the same day, tens of thousands of people were killed in an earthquake in Iran, but the headline in *Yedi'ot Aharonot* on Sunday read, "The Company Commander Instructed His Soldiers: Shoot the Demonstrators." Israeli media's interest in us was a mirror image of how it had ignored us up to that moment.

The sudden spotlight placed us in a problematic position: standing on a platform we didn't really choose, feeling the pain from our friend's injury, and yet still wanting to disseminate information about the injustice that had caused us to cut through the fence in the first place. Much as with our attitude toward Shimon Peres and Yossi Sarid—two politicians who, within the space of two bullets, went from being our ideological enemies to our self-appointed loyal spokesmen—we had also accumulated hostility toward the corporate media. But when the platform was given us, and with it seemingly the opportunity to change the public agenda, it was difficult for us to refuse.

Since we don't all define ourselves as anarchists, but all agree on an anarchist way of working—without leaders and led, without hierarchy and with the maximum participation of all members of the group—we attempted to share the work of speaking to different media programs. Invitations flowed to us from every direction, allowing almost all of us to make a live appearance. Cheska spoke on *What's Burning*, Anat on *Erev Hadash*, Liad on the Russian channel, Jonathan on *London and Kirschenbaum*, Shelly on *Politica*, and Nimrod on *Seven-Thirty*.

We practiced interview simulations, sharing our experience with one another. We tried to give the media what they wanted ("So why were you shot at? How did you feel when they fired? Aren't you afraid of suicide bombers? Can you arrange an exclusive interview with Gil Na'amati for me?"), but also talk about shootings and protesters although not just Jewish Israeli protesters, the closed gate at Mas'ha and not just the shooting, the harm done by the fence in general and not just Mas'ha, the policy of apartheid and ethnic cleansing and not just the fence, and maybe even anti-Zionism and anarchism and not just Palestine.

That week, Eyal Ofer published a story in the *Ha'aretz* weekend magazine about Hani Amer's fenced-in yard in

Mas'ha, and Rogel Alfer published a chilling confession about his basic training in 1985 and "the rotten products of an occupying society." They knew they were faced with leftist activists, said Alfer, and acted accordingly. On Channel 10, Rino Tzror offered an in-depth exposé that pulled the ground out from under the Israeli army spokesperson's lies. A camera, we already knew, is an effective weapon in the war for truth. We had at least three on the ground. At the press conference we convened in an attempt to confront the army's lies, we presented our own debrief, which was based on the video footage. Representatives of all Israeli media outlets came to our press conference. For a few days, the anarchist kid who was constantly up for expulsion from school became the most popular kid in class.

In response to the media interest in the findings we presented, the army was quick to publish its own debrief on the event, and the next day the findings were published in the papers opposite one another: the anarchists' versus the army's versions.

Media interest in us as well as in the circumstances that brought us to cut the fence continued. In *Yedi'ot Aharonot*, Yigal Serna told the story of gate no. 1549—the gate at Mas'ha that we broke through when it was left closed in contravention of the army's own promises, preventing farmers from reaching their lands. Serna even mentioned the connection between anarchism and veganism. Meron Benvenisti outdid them all when he wrote in *Ha'aretz* about "the intellectual challenge that anarchists place before a society that accords 'a Jewish State' absolute and sacred value, and worships 'laws' as if they embody, solely by the virtue of being legislated, supreme moral and social values." Benvenisti determined that "a little anarchism won't hurt," which to me clarified that the public relations damage of choosing the name anarchists was worthwhile.

Other fruits were reaped later: ten days after the incident, an editorial was published in *Ha'aretz* under the title "The Harm Done by the Fence," and Akiva Eldar did an exposé about the meager punishments given to soldiers who injured or killed innocent Palestinians. All of these did not make me forget Gil Na'amati's pain, but the accumulating archive certainly added meaning to the price he paid and continues to pay. No longer will anyone be able to say, "I didn't know." After a few days, as it goes with the corporate media, new topics rose to the agenda and things calmed down.

A year later, not a single journalist was interested in the investigation findings submitted by the military police to the attorney general. No journalist would investigate how it happened that the soldier who shot Na'amati advanced through the military ranks, without anyone being taken to task for it. Meanwhile, Na'amati's legs still do not allow him to walk.

It's hard to overestimate the publicity and public benefit that this incident had for the opposition to the fence's construction. Without diminishing the attempts and successes that preceded December 26, 2003, this moment represented a real turnaround in attitudes. Now a position exists in the public sphere that must be considered, mentioned, and given voice. The consensus has been fractured. Security reasoning can no longer silence all protest.

Minister of Justice Yosef Lapid's concerns, the rulings by the Hague International Court, and the Israeli Supreme Court's decision that disqualified the fence in its current route are further milestones in the long, exhausting trail from the raving fringes to the heart of the consensus.

The fact that Israelis are partners in the daily resistance actions against the fence along its dispossessing route is no longer a secret. And yet it seems to me that for most of us who show up at demonstrations and actions along the wall, media interest is an important tool in reducing violence toward the protesters, even though it is certainly not an end in itself.

In Mas'ha, Beit Surik, Budrus, Deir Balut, Beit Likia, A-Ram, and other villages, we are creating, here and now, with our own bodies, an alternative community based on shared fate as well as cross-national and cross-ethnic solidarity. This change is taking place with or without the media spotlight, which will certainly shine again when the first Israeli protester is killed, and will again go out within a few days.

—Uri Ayalon

Dykes and the Holy War

As a queer-anarchist activist from Israel, I am quite often confronted with questions concerning the engagement of queer groups or individuals in the Palestinian struggle against the Israeli apartheid regime. How could I, as a queer and an anarchist, fight for the establishment of a state where the powers of occupation will just change hands, and will erect new and old oppression? What do we have to do with a national movement that is reconstructing the same national ideals we are working to dismantle in our own society? I will try to examine these questions here, and look at the role of solidarity and joint struggle from a queer-anarchist perspective.

Maybe the most important point to clarify at the beginning is the role that the occupation since 1967 and oppression of the Palestinian minority in Israel since 1948 (1948 Palestinians) both play in Israeli Jewish society.

The state of Israel, which claims to be a "Jewish and democratic state" that upholds equal rights for all it inhabitants, is having great difficulties maintaining its democratic aspirations in light of its colonialist and religious nature. It is widely recognized that the democratic rights and freedoms of members from even the "more privileged groups" in Israel are suffering from the decades-old ongoing occupation and the social reality that emerged from it. The need for national unity in the face of ever-coming wars, the rapid militarization of a society that needs to control every step of three million Palestinians, and the demographic war that needs to be waged against the Palestinian uterus takes its toll on minority groups in Israel, and harms all emancipation struggles like the feminist movement, LGBTQ community, workers' organizations, ecological campaigns, Ethiopian and Mizrahi groups, and many others. In a society that is in a constant state of emergency, it is difficult to fight for social justice or even speak about it.

The history of the LGBTQ rights movement in Israel serves as an example for the influences of major political events on a specific struggle for equal rights. The existence of gay and lesbian groups since the 1970s, together with several openly gay artists, poets, and filmmakers, did create a small circle of understanding and tolerance for sexual minorities, but no one could ignore the fact that the biggest and strongest wave of LGBTQ political action and successes took place in the 1990s, particularly after the election of Yitzhak Rabin (together with the big electoral achievement of Meretz, the Zionist liberal-Left party) and the beginning of the Oslo "peace process" with the Palestinian Liberation Organization. As unrealistic and false as they were, the hopes that the failed peace process raised among the Israeli public—hopes for a real democratic state, an end to religious coercion, and a new Middle East—gave the push that the LGBTQ community needed in order to gain recognition and legal achievements. The second Intifada, catalyzed by the reemergence of religious control, nationalism, and militarism, stopped these processes, and one might argue, also led to the huge backlash and wave of homophobic violence in the streets as well as the media that was sparked by the attempt to hold an international gay pride parade in West Jerusalem.

Thus it is clear for many political activists in progressive circles that the national conflict currently blocks any kind of radical progress, disables coalition building, and is being used and intensified quite often in order to silence social conflicts inside Israel (one can find a similar phenomenon within Palestinian society, where the struggle against Israeli occupation is being used by some reactionary groups to silence social and feminist critics). The first step for radical social and feminist change in Israeli society must then be an end to the occupation, but what does that really mean?

The Occupation Never Stops

"When the occupation ends. . . . " How many times have we said this to ourselves, fantasizing over a future paradise, while becoming more and more cynical and disillusioned with each passing year. Today we know better. The occupation is not going to end; it is here to stay. Two truths stand as I make this statement: first, the end of the occupation with a two-state solution based on the 1967 borders is unrealistic, and second, the occupation is not just "the occupation of 1967" but instead a much broader situation existing under the control of the state of Israel. A solution comprised of two national states coexisting side by side as equals is today a sad joke, and maybe it always was. This much-endorsed solution was hijacked from its progressive supporters many years ago (only the Communist Party in Israel demanded "two states for two people" in the 1980s), and distorted in order to legitimize the apartheid of the twenty-first century. We now know how these two states will look: barbed-wired Bantustans surrounded by the same big military camp known as Israel. The occupation will just continue under the new Orwellian definition of peace process and a false independence.

But opposition to the two-state solution is not based solely on its implementation being impossible. It also is premised on the fact that it ignores numerous aspects and existing problems. The occupation of 1967 cannot be understood as an external problem, an invader's colonial fight. The occupation of 1967 is not an external problem disconnected from Israel's internal problems. Apartheid and the politics of occupation are the very basis of the state of Israel: the ethnic cleansing of eight hundred thousand Palestinians in 1948 and continued refusal to allow their return; the barefaced discrimination and ever-increasing police violence against 1948 Palestinians; and the need to settle and protect the land from the illegal people, Judaize the periphery, and wage a demographic war—all these take place in what is called Israel and not in what is known as the occupied territories. The occupation doesn't stop at the checkpoint. It is all around us, and thus there is no "here" and "there." Israel is the occupation.

The Necessity of the Joint Struggle

The struggle against occupation and apartheid must be waged, not because it is the first step toward the revolution, but rather simply because daily war crimes and mass human rights violations are unacceptable, regardless of whether the victims of these crimes are revolutionary anarchists or hardworking, poor conservative Muslims. The fact that the oppressed sector is not the perfect revolutionary subject (if there is such a thing) does not in any way diminish my obligation to stand alongside it against the state—my state—which is curtailing its basic rights. This should be enough to explain why one should fight fiercely against the occupation. Yet fighting against something is never enough; we need to fight *for*, for a different future, for what we think is the best solution for all people to live with—but what is it?

One of the most critical issues for Israel's radical Left, especially since the beginning of the Intifada, is the joint political work of Palestinians and Israeli Jews. This could be understood as a reaction to the racist politics that Israel stands for: total separation between Israelis and Palestinians, be it with walls (in 1948 Israel and the West Bank), checkpoints, and apartheid roads, or through separate schools, racist and religious marriage laws, and the racist harassment of "Arab-looking" people at the entrance of every mall, restaurant, or club. In such a blatantly racist atmosphere, the most radical act is to break this separation by demonstrating together with Palestinians, living together, talking to each other, loving and caring for each other—even making love with each other. It is not well recognized what a strong and amazing emotional effect meeting Palestinians for the first time as equal partners in a struggle, or even becoming friends with them, has on an Israeli Jew. Nor is it understood how important it is to have these contacts in order to challenge our own racist and Orientalist attitudes, and destroy the "clash of civilizations" theory (I can personally admit that sometimes it was only my emotional connection to my several Palestinian friends that kept me sane under the constant wave of racist and nationalist propaganda). To come together, to live together— Ta'ayush in Arabic—is simultaneously our means and ends.

Liberation as a Process

Bringing down the borders of nation and race might be the ultimate goal, but the situation is a bit more challenging than that. Palestinians, as an ethnic group suffering from national oppression as well as devoid of their own self-determination and state, are fighting against their oppression in the most common and familiar way: leading a national liberation struggle in hope of achieving an independent, national state. The fact that people forced to live under racist or nationalist oppression merge into a national group as a way to fight for their rights, along with the sad fact that almost all national liberation struggles create new oppressive systems, should not be alien to us as Israeli Jews.

But what should we do as anarchists in this struggle? What are we actually fighting for, and with whom? Are we trying to be a part of this "national liberation process," as some Israeli radical-Left activists do, and see ourselves as Jewish Palestinians? Or do we believe that national liberation is just a point one should go through, one step forward, and that the day it ends victoriously (and another good question would be, What does the end of a national liberation struggle in Palestine mean?) will also be the day that the exploited Palestinian masses start the social revolution together with their Jewish working-class brothers and sisters? Or is it perhaps totally irrelevant what we think or want because we are a part of the colonialist society, and as such should only offer our unconditional solidarity with the goals and needs of the oppressed sector?

These questions, although cynically phrased, are not without merit. National liberation is always ambiguous: it is the liberation from colonialist oppression yet at the same time the construction of new models of oppression and exploitation, and it is exactly within this ambivalent situation that we need to choose our path. This becomes even more complicated when we talk about a colonialist situation that cannot be dealt with by driving the colonialist powers back to their home countries. Rather, it is a matter of decolonizing the settler society, taking the Israelis into account not only as the current oppressors but also as a people that deserves the same freedoms and rights as all other peoples in the region.

The joint Palestinian-Israeli struggle—the fight against the wall in which AAtW participates, or the many campaigns in which Ta'ayush supported Palestinian communities in the occupied territories or 1948 Israel—seems to be the best way to tackle the many contradictions we face in a politically productive way. The joint work of Israelis and Palestinians is in this sense one of the goals, and maybe the most important goal, of every campaign we take part in—be it resisting the wall, housing demolitions, or army invasions. Through this work, we deconstruct the racist foundations of the conflict. An Israeli taking part in a Palestinian demonstration, risking their life and body in the face of brutal army oppression, is challenging not only the basic understandings of the Israeli soldier (soldiers ask us quite often, before or after shooting at us, if we are not afraid to get killed inside the villages by their Palestinian residents) but also those of the Palestinian farmer who meets Israelis only as their oppressor.

Naturally, the coming together of Palestinians and Israelis is not an easy task for those on either side. We must remember that many cultural, political, and social differences exist alongside our positions of power within this conflict—positions we cannot simply ignore out of the hope or belief that we are all just equal partners in a struggle. The struggle to change and challenge Palestinian culture with its patriarchal, militarist, and homophobic elements is not our task but instead that of our Palestinian comrades, to whom we must offer our solidarity—first and foremost by lifting the weight of the occupation from their shoulders, and by fighting those same elements in our own society. Liberation is always a process, and it can evolve and intensify only by removing the biggest obstacle that stands in its way.

—Yossi Bartal

"Hey Babe,
Hope You're Not in Jail"

As dissenting Israelis in this emotionally charged landscape, we almost daily meet differences and difficulties with nonaligned friends and family. Rarely do we agree. Most of the time we disagree. Sometimes there is shouting, and occasionally there are tears. And there are times when we altogether stop being friends. What we do as activists is not purely political; it is also personal. Whether face-to-face or on Facebook, our political activism eventually comes up.

It can be difficult and emotional discussing the occupation along with the general situation in Israel and Palestine. I, for one, get frustrated and sometimes feel guilty. I will move heaven and earth to make it to a demonstration in one particular village. Like most of the activists I know, I spend money and time getting to meetings, gatherings, and demonstrations. A single phone call, and we will rush to wherever we are needed. We will make a hundred calls trying to get someone out of detention, or spend hours outside a police station waiting for their release or in court. This can, occasionally, leave little time for me to invest in my relationships with my few nonaligned friends. Solidarity may be defined as "an entire union or consolidation of interests and responsibilities; fellowship; community." For me it is also identifying with others' pain and wanting to do something about it. But how do we explain this to someone who is nonaligned? How do we convey to them its importance? Should we try to convey it at all?

Here, I look at the relationships and dynamics that we have with our nonaligned friends and family, how we deal (or don't deal) with them, and our feelings, realizations, and conclusions around all that. What language do we use when talking to those in our lives who are not aligned? Do we lie, tell the truth, or tell a partial truth about our solidarity activities? What responsibility or obligation do we have as conscientious Israelis to talk to as well as raise awareness among our friends and family? And at what point (if at all) do we no longer feel the need, nor the point, of "preaching to the unconverted"?

For those of us who have friends who are nonaligned, the relationship varies. Many people have friends who may not be directly involved in solidarity with the Palestinian struggle but instead are involved in other struggles—human rights, animal rights, housing rights, and refugee rights, to name but a few. Some find their way, through other solidarity activities, to standing with us at demonstrations in the occupied Palestinian territories. And then there are some of us who still have friends, from home and childhood, who are nonaligned not only with regards to anarchism or the Palestinian cause but also in terms of actively working for the rights of others in general. Some may have found their way to the social housing protests of the summer, yet have since returned to (whatever it is they consider) a "normal life."

It would be helpful to clarify the term nonaligned at this point. I am referring not only to those who do not identify themselves as anarchists but also those who do not identify with the Palestinian popular struggle. Then there are those who are nonaligned politically but verbally express support for dismantling the settlements, and recognize the overt racism and separation in our societies, although they excuse the occupation using Zionist (both left and right) arguments—even though they may not themselves identify as Zionists. The microdefinitions and identities of our friends and families are as complicated as the political, religious, and cultural identities of our society as a whole. As a result, while seeking to convey the complexity of our relationships with family and friends, I'm not claiming to offer a definitive answer or conclusion here. This piece is about our experiences, thoughts, and realizations, and aims to shed light on an intimate aspect of our activism in Israel and Palestine.

Relationships and Dynamics

It is hard to convey our situation to outsiders. To put it lightly, support for the Palestinian popular struggle is not a position held by the majority in this country. A fellow activist and close friend says she uses the metaphor of "coming out" to convey the emotional dynamics of confronting family and friends with her views and actions.

Like others, I have gradually lost contact with most of my friends from home. Some of us cannot deal with the confrontations and so we drift apart. As we go on, the gap widens between us and our nonaligned environment. Those who are still close to me know just about everything. Those I lost have known me for a long time, and my actions were not entirely new to them. Their only "criticism" was that I had become more *extreme*, and to be fair I have, only I use the term *radical* and have no qualms about it. My best friends nevertheless worry about me. Whether conscious or not, sometimes their reactions to my beliefs or actions are insensitive. When Mustafa Tamimi was killed by a tear gas canister shot to the head at close range, I asked a friend if she had heard about it. Her immediate reaction was, "Yes! And I wish you lot would stop going on about it!" My first question to her was going to be, "That's interesting, which other friends do you have who have posted about it? I would love to meet them!" but instead I told her I was there at the time. Her tone immediately changed. She asked me how I was and what had happened. But some point she asked me why I keep putting myself in these extreme situations, and why I don't take a break. I asked her, Is the occupation taking a break?

She worries. They all worry. They are my friends and family, and it makes sense. It's natural. Her immediate reaction, her first thought, however, was why we kept posting and talking about the death of a Palestinian killed in cold blood. If it had been a friend of ours, if it had been a Jew, would she have reacted in the same way? I don't know, but the nagging feeling in my stomach makes me wonder.

I am one of the lucky ones; my parents, particularly my father, are supportive and as activists themselves have taken part in demonstrations. They boycott goods from settlements and support a Palestinian family from Jenin needing medical care in Israel. They have bailed me out of jail and comforted me after difficult days, and they always know when to step back and trust that I know what I'm doing. We have only ever had one massive falling out over my opinions and actions. When the "flytilla" of May 2011 was on its way to Israel, I showed no restraint at expressing my support, but in an unusual sign of emotion my mother told me that she would throw me out of the house if I did anything that "threatened the existence of Israel." I have come home high as a kite, drunk as a fish, and stayed out on numerous nights without letting them know where, and she never reacted like that. After a heated exchange, she apologized. The only reason I tell this particular story is because this is the worst it has ever gotten in my house, and only a few weeks later she looked on as I was arrested for trying to stop the separation wall from being built. Her emotional survival mechanisms and attachment to this country are the source of her passionate reactions. She is not a nationalist, she despises the current government, but she takes it personally when I attack Zionism. She rationalizes it as a disjuncture between what *is* and what *ought to be*, "what is going on now isn't Zionism," "historically Zionism meant. . . ." Although to be fair, I also have noticed clearly how my own process as an activist has had a ripple effect on those close to me, and I am not unique in this. Other friends I know have the same story, where their family has become more radicalized, aware, and active as a result of their own actions. But this process seems to happen only when family or friends are open to it.

Yet not everyone has hippies for parents. My friend Tomer and her family have clearly opposing views, and therefore she is "all for keeping peace at home" so that she can continue doing solidarity work. She says, "If I don't have . . . the material support of my family, I cannot do what I do. . . . What is the point in killing my basic means of survival?" This means her activism remains an unapproachable subject. During Operation Cast Lead in Gaza, she sat with her father when it was announced that a UN building had been targeted and forty people had been killed. "It's not enough," he commented. "Now he's a very nice person actually," she says. But "in the fervor of the moment, he and I don't have a lot to talk about."

I know people who have effectively left their families and opted not to engage with them on anything other than a very basic level. I also know those who, out of no choice of their own, having been treated as so different, feel that they can no longer continue in the family unit dynamic. At the time of this writing, my uncle and his wife are not talking to me. In every phone call my mother has with him, he brings up my political activity, and she talks to him, tries to explain. But as an Israeli living abroad, caught up in the Zionist narrative and the news, he neither knows nor wants to know what is actually happening here. Like many others, he will also attack the other side as a way to avoid confronting our role in creating the problem.

In so many ways, our nonaligned friends and family are disconnected from the Palestinians and the military rule under which they suffer. They spend years being "taught" to dehumanize, and fail to see the obvious racism and discrimination in their own words. I see it as a collective survival tactic. The self-suppression and denial are ways for them to stay sane. Self-inflicted ignorance and innocence are ways for them to stop from breaking. So how can we relate to such an emotional state? How can we facilitate a "breaking" process without breaking the relationship? Can we ever make them come around to our side?

Yes, I feel a breaking process is needed. I have the tiniest bit of hope left that Jewish society can wake up from its drugged stupor of nationalism and fear, and realize that it is we who have become the abusers, that we are no longer the victim, and start to do something about it so we can all live in a safer, better world.

Friends or Enemies?

An activist friend of mine told me that within his circle of friends from home, he is considered a radical left-winger—except that they don't even know the half of it. He shares his opinions with them, but not his actions. They don't know that he joins demonstrations every Friday or raises money. I questioned him on this, asking whether he doesn't feel like he's hiding a part of himself from them, or even lying to them. He said, "I would rather keep them as friends than lose them as enemies." I questioned him on this as well, curious to know if he didn't feel that they miss out on knowing a part of him—a sort of "lying by omission" where keeping the peace takes precedent. But it's the same with me. My nearest and dearest have no idea *how* involved I am in the boycott, divestment, and sanctions movement because I know what kind of reactions it would invoke. It seems we are left with three choices: keep our friends and lie, tell the truth and lose them, or tell the truth and hope that one day they will come around.

Social networking sites are another story. There, I filter myself. I have a list of about a hundred people who see everything that I post and discuss. The rest see something different. Why do I do this? Because I cannot deal with the racist, demeaning, or ignorant reactions from people. So I don't tell my closest friends everything that I get up to. It has become easier not to. I have tried doing the political talk with them, but they take the conversation to the potential negative impact that going to weekly protests could have, and confuse it with caring for me. They tell me I am an extremist, whereas I call it radical. They tell me that I talk in slogans, whereas I tell them what I think. They tell me that I am not from here; I tell them this is my home.

Nevertheless the dynamics do change. Even while writing and researching for this piece, my relationships have developed with my closest friends. I'm self-censoring less and less. Family and friends have come to me with stories they have heard, and I tell them about what I see and experience, about the expansion of settlements and brutality of the Israeli army reactions at protests. My job now means that supporting the Palestinian popular struggle and fighting the occupation have become integral parts of my life, and if someone is going to be an intimate part of my life, then they are going to be exposed to these aspects of it.

The discourse, like our relationships, is neither fixed nor static. A friend of mine suggests a change of tactics. "Perhaps we should just agree with them, tell them they are right! And then invite them out." Invite them to a demonstration, to a village in the West Bank. Invite them to meet a man whose house will be surrounded by a fence because he refuses to move from where the route of the wall is being built. Invite them to meet Palestinian farmers whose land is being stolen and whose olive trees have been uprooted. Some go as far as to turn their own birthday into a political act by having a tour in a forest park that was once a Palestinian village. And then there are the times when we come to our families and friends expressing exhaustion, sadness, and rage, and are told, "Well then, stop going, stop doing it." There is a limit to how many times you can explain that this is not a solution, that not going and not standing there in solidarity is not an option. So you just stop explaining.

An Obligation to Debate?

At demonstrations we are there in solidarity, pure and simple. We are there supporting the antioccupation movement; we do not set the agenda. But what about when we are not in a demonstration or solidarity action in Palestine? When it is not a Friday out in the occupied territories? According to some, we can and therefore should be talking to Israeli society, to our friends and family who may or may not be fighting in the IDF, living in a settlement, or burying their heads in the sand.

For instance, when in interrogation, or standing opposite the soldiers or police, these are people we might know—family, family of friends, friends, or friends of friends. We could stand there and talk to them, ask them questions, sometimes yell at them too, even if they are not allowed to respond (although some at times do). Generally, though, there can be no interaction between us. When we sit in interrogation after an arrest, sometimes the investigator will try a new friendly tactic, telling you the questioning is over and that he "just wants to know why you are doing this." I, like others, tell them the same thing. "You want to know? Then let's go out for a coffee or beer, but while we are in this position of you the interrogator and me the one under investigation, I reserve the right to remain silent."

Do we have a responsibility or obligation as conscientious Israelis to talk to, convince, and debate with Israeli society? In many ways we are privileged to be Jewish and mainly middle class, and as much as we may be averse to admitting it, we speak the same language and have a similar culture to our nonaligned friends and family. Some feel that we should be talking to other Israelis as much as possible, as long as we have not been killed or totally silenced. They can listen to us. We speak the same language, dress similarly, and have grown up together. Yet the majority of those I spoke to give similar answers. First, there is little faith that Israeli society will ever change its discourse, which is based on fear and propaganda, especially in view of the government's increasingly right-wing and religious policies. Second, there are the mental and emotional limitations we have in dealing with the harsh and difficult reactions we often receive. We each have and set our own boundaries, and some do not feel the need for, nor are they capable of, putting themselves through the experience of an emotionally charged debate.

And then there was also an answer given by one activist, but an answer that I share and believe many of us will identify with. Yoni told me that one day at a particularly violent demonstration, a couple of Palestinian activists approached him and asked why he was there rather than talking to people in Tel Aviv about what is going on. Yoni told me that "being considered an extremist has made it harder to engage." He felt he was most effective at the beginning of his journey, when he and his friends spoke the same language, and they could better identify with him. I had a similar experience as I was walking back to the van from one of my first demonstrations in the West Bank. A local Palestinian farmer stopped me and bluntly asked what I was doing there. Why, for example, was I not in Tel Aviv talking to Israelis, or demonstrating outside the Knesset or prime minister's house? I did not have a decent answer for him, but I did not go to another demonstration for three years, although I did not confront Israeli society either. I just left the country. My friend Hila explained when asked about this, "It is an obligation to resist, to fight the occupation and stand in solidarity; this is a principle. But talking to Jews and facing Israelis is a method—one that you choose like any other."

Nonetheless, there it is: Palestinian partners are asking us to show our solidarity by talking to Israelis; they see it as having political value. If our understanding is that this is their struggle, that we are supporting it, then it is important that we as Israeli activists address the questions raised by our Palestinian partners, and perhaps heed this call.

Ultimately each one of us does what we can, to our own and best ability. It is understandable when you have been isolated from the majority of society, and when every debate turns into an emotionally exhausting and highly charged argument, that people do give up.

Realizations and Conclusions

It is clear that this is a difficult issue and an ambitious subject to tackle. This piece is not based on academic studies or books I have read. It is about people's experience, in a small attempt to hash out some picture of our lives here.

Our environment, our relationships, and the discourses we use are dynamic. As time passes, I have become more confident in my opinions and the role that I have in the world, especially here in Palestine/Israel. The confidence and calm assurance that I am fighting the good fight means that I can use compassion and not just passion, empathy and not anger, when talking to my friends and family. This is the approach I will try to use in my intimate relationships. The facts and experiences do not change; it is only how I relate them to others that is being refined and developed. I remember clearly the day my father began using the word apartheid to describe the reality here with no appre-hension. Even if things move only a little bit, it becomes a big deal.

I do wonder what makes me different from them. If they're so curious, why don't they come and see what is go-ing on with their own eyes? I have no satisfactory answer, but these questions do occupy my mind. How does one explain that due to basic human rights violations, restric-tions on movement, blatant landgrabbing, and violation of international law, our solidarity is anchored in a deep con-viction about right and wrong? Acquiescence is simply not possible. This is something that brings the aligned together. We do not have to defend, argue about, or explain to one another why it is we do what we do. It is clear to us why.

Perhaps our successful relationships with nonaligned friends and family are a sort of rebellion in their own right—rebelling against the idea that we cannot hold op-posing opinions and still have healthy relationships. My activist comrades, close confidants, family, and nonaligned friends are all part of my community. They are my support network, within which I can function as a better activist. I gather strength from their support. I could not do what I do without them.

—Ruth Edmonds

Another Land

This text is both personal and political, and in it I want to sum up a little more than a year of intensive activity within the framework of AAtW. The group's activity affected my life, my identity, the spaces of my personal and political activity, and the way I perceive them. Now, as I sit to write this piece, I look back and wonder at what point in time and space the decision was made in my heart to "become an activist," in a radical way, in spaces that until then were conceived as "far," "threatening," and "dangerous" in my mind, and with people that until a little more than a year ago I didn't know at all, or knew only superficially. I try here to inject a little order into the vast experiences I've had over the last year, and place them in a coherent narrative in time and space. It is perhaps a personal-spatial autobiography of border crossing and activism.

Becoming an Activist

In December 2008, the Israeli army began Operation Cast Lead, a war against a civilian population in the Gaza Strip during which more than a thousand civilians were killed, among them hundreds of children. At the end of May 2010, the famous flotillas made their way toward Gaza with the goal of breaking the siege. The army's attack on one of the boats ended with the murder of nine Turkish activists along with a wave of pseudo-patriotic support for the army and criminal Israeli policy, both in the media and Israeli public discourse. I was opposed to the siege of Gaza, furious about Operation Cast Lead, and felt nausea and disgust toward the public discourse following the flotilla. Despite this, I made do with posting comments and Facebook statuses as well as participating once in a demonstration in front of the Ministry of Defense in Tel Aviv, and again felt that I was not doing enough. I knew it was possible to do more, but didn't know exactly what. I was afraid to go to Bil'in; the village seemed distant in my mind, threatening and frightening, but I heard about demonstrations in Sheikh Jarrah in East Jerusalem. At that time, the protests in Sheikh Jarrah had been going on for about a year in opposition to evictions of Palestinian residents from their houses. I decided to go there with a friend one Friday afternoon at the beginning of 2011. That was my first real border crossing, a demonstration in a Palestinian neighborhood in East Jerusalem, in which Jews and Arabs participated together.

We stood there, on the side of the road crossing Sheikh Jarrah, holding signs and repeating slogans that another demonstrator yelled loudly through a megaphone in Hebrew and Arabic: "From Sheikh Jarrah to Bil'in, free, free Palestine," "Police and border police—get out of

Sheikh Jarrah now," and others. But one slogan that repeated itself with minor variations caught my ears in a special way: "Sheikh Jarrah, don't despair—we'll stop the occupation." This slogan was repeated, each time with the name of a new place—once Bil'in, once Ma'asara, once Beit Omar, once Ni'ilin, and once Nabi Saleh.

As I sat on the bus with my friend on our way back to Tel Aviv, I mentioned to her that I'd heard about the demonstrations in Bil'in and had also heard something about Ni'ilin, but that I didn't know the other names I'd heard at the protest. I wrote down the names and places in my notebook, and when I returned home I immediately checked name after name on Google, and was amazed to discover that indeed in all those villages, for months and years, Israeli supporters—mostly from the group AAtW—had joined Palestinian demonstrators. I discovered that although I customarily read the paper every day (an Israeli paper in Hebrew, of course), and was generally conversant in world news, politics, and culture, I actually didn't know what was going on an hour's drive from my own home. Agitated by these revelations, I decided I needed to go out to these demonstrations and see them with my own eyes.

Within a week, I had participated in a demonstration in Ma'asara. It was the first demonstration I'd attended that Palestinians had organized and in which most participants were Palestinian. For the first time in my life I stood opposite Israeli army soldiers, together with Palestinian demonstrators. This was a jarring experience, from the Palestinian flags carried by some of the participants to the gas canisters used by the soldiers to disperse the protest. Nonetheless, the following week I went to Beit Ommar, and the next one I went to Bil'in. Nabi Saleh and Ni'ilin took a bit longer, but in the end I went to those villages too.

From that moment onward I can say with certainty that my life changed. This shift was reflected in how I began to "spend" my Fridays. I stopped passing them by relaxing in Tel Aviv with friends at home or in cafés, as I'd done prior to this point, and started spending Fridays at West Bank demonstrations, every week at a different village. The change was not just a spatial-geographic one; it was also social and cultural. It had to do with the people who I traveled to the demonstrations with, the Palestinians I met in the occupied villages, and my exposure to these Palestinians' culture and language. The change was also and mainly one of consciousness: I felt as though I had crossed a border that wasn't just physical or sociocultural but also one of consciousness and understanding—leaving behind a large part of my previous life.

One of the immediate insights from this drastic transformation was the understanding that something big had existed for some time and at a short distance from Tel Aviv, without my knowing it. This caused me many pangs of conscience, not to mention feelings of guilt and shame. I understood that I was not the first (and would not be the last) to feel this way. It was in itself a border crossing—a symbolic border that separated good from bad, forbidden from allowed, enemy from ally. Physical places I'd considered dangerous quickly became spaces within which I felt great comfort. People who for years I perceived as threatening now became partners and allies, whose villages and homes demonstrations and protests—and do not include tear gas or anything life endangering.

I met S., a young Palestinian guy from Ramallah, at one of my first demonstrations in Bil'in. We met at a training given by one of the experienced demonstrators beforehand, and became friends thereafter. We met a few more times in Bil'in, and every time, S. invited me to come visit his home in Ramallah. I had doubts, mostly because I was afraid of traveling to Ramallah. Despite the physical and mental borders I had already crossed, and despite the fact that social borders were part of this, I was still hesitant to accept the invitation. But indeed I met S. on a Friday afternoon in Bil'in, and right after the demonstration traveled with him and another friend to Ramallah.

S. took us on a tour of the city—a tour I didn't think was possible to complete, since Ramallah is in what's called Area-A and entry to Israeli Jews is prohibited by law. We visited the Mukata'a (the offices of the administrative center of the Palestinian National Authority) and Yasser Arafat's grave, and then sat to eat dinner in a local restaurant's enchanting garden. On our way from the restaurant to a short rest at S.'s home, we stopped at the highest point in the city from which, as S. said, "on a clear day you can see Tel Aviv." How near and yet how far. In the evening we went out to two popular bars, drank Taybeh beer, and had fun. The next day we traveled the winding way to Tel Aviv. Seemingly there is nothing special about a weekend with friends in a city that is an hour and a half drive from home, but in fact there is much more to it. If not for the changes in my life that began with joining the demonstrations and activism, it is reasonable to assume that I wouldn't have found myself spending a weekend in a city that it is illegal for me to enter, together with Palestinian friends, in places that are culturally distant from the places I frequented prior to this time. The ride to Ramallah also constituted a border crossing—a physical border, a cultural and social border, and one of consciousness. I hope that more Israelis get the opportunity to visit there. Only good can come of an acquaintance with the people who live in the place from which on a clear day you can see Tel Aviv.

—Chen Misgav
Translated by Rona Even

Credits for Anarchist Interventions

Uri Gordon

Uri is an Israeli activist, teacher, and writer. He has been active with the Negev Coexistence Forum for Civil Equality, and in global networks including Indymedia and Peoples' Global Action. He teaches politics at Loughborough University in the United Kingdom, and is the author of the *Anarchy Alive! Anti-authoritarian Politics from Practice to Theory* (Pluto Press, 2008) as well as numerous articles on the theory and practice of contemporary anarchism. His work has been translated into ten languages.

Ohal Grietzer

Ohal is a visual artist and composer, currently residing in New York. She is a graduate of Goldsmiths, University of London, where she researched the use of irony in politics and obtained a master's degree in anthropology. She has been an activist with Anarchists Against the Wall and Boycott! Supporting the Palestinian BDS Call from Within.

Institute for Anarchist Studies

The IAS, a nonprofit foundation established in 1996, aims to support the development of anarchism by creating spaces for independent, politically engaged scholarship that explores social domination and reconstructive visions of a free society. All IAS projects strive to encourage public intellectuals and collective self-reflection within revolutionary and/or movement contexts. To this end, the IAS awards grants twice a year to radical writers and translators worldwide, and has funded some ninety projects over the years by authors from numerous countries, including Argentina, Lebanon, Canada, Chile, Ireland, Nigeria, Germany, South Africa, and the United States. It also publishes the online and print journal *Perspectives on Anarchist Theory* as well as the new Lexicon pamphlet series, organizes the Renewing the Anarchist Tradition conference and anarchist theory tracks, offers the Mutual Aid Speakers List, and collaborates on this book series, among other projects. The IAS is part of a larger movement seeking to create a nonhierarchical society. It is internally democratic and works in solidarity with people around the globe who share its values. The IAS is completely supported by donations from anarchists and other antiauthoritarians—like you—and/or their projects, with any contributions exclusively funding grants and IAS operating expenses; for more information or to contribute to the work of the IAS, see http://www.anarchist-studies.org/.

AK Press

AK Press is a worker-run collective that publishes and distributes radical books, visual and audio media, and other material. We're small: a dozen people who work long hours for short money, because we believe in what we do. We're anarchists, which is reflected both in the books we provide and the way we organize our business. Decisions at

AK Press are made collectively, from what we publish, to what we distribute and how we structure our labor. All the work, from sweeping floors to answering phones, is shared. When the telemarketers call and ask, "who's in charge?" the answer is: everyone. Our goal isn't profit (although we do have to pay the rent). Our goal is supplying radical words and images to as many people as possible. The books and other media we distribute are published by independent presses, not the corporate giants. We make them widely available to help you make positive (or hell, revolutionary) changes in the world. For more information on AK Press, or to place an order, see http://www.akpress.org/.

Justseeds Artists' Cooperative

Justseeds Artists' Cooperative is a decentralized community of twenty-two artists who have banded together to both sell their work, and collaborate with and support each other and social movements. Our Web site is not just a place to shop but also a destination to find out about current events in radical art and culture. We regularly collaborate on exhibitions and group projects as well as produce graphics and culture for social justice movements. We believe in the power of personal expression in concert with collective action to transform society. For more information on Justseeds Artists' Cooperative or to order work, see http://www.justseeds.org/.

Anarchist Intervention Series

Support **AK Press!**

AK Press is one of the world's largest and most productive anarchist publishing houses. We're entirely worker-run & democratically managed. We

operate without a corporate structure—no boss, no managers, no bullshit. We publish close to twenty books every year, and distribute thousands of other titles published by other like-minded independent presses and projects from around the globe.

The Friends of AK program is a way that you can directly contribute to the continued existence of AK Press, and ensure that we're able to keep publishing great books just like this one! Friends pay $25 a month directly into our publishing account ($30 for Canada, $35 for international), and receive a copy of every book AK Press publishes for the duration of their membership! Friends also receive a discount on anything they order from our website or buy at a table: 50% on AK titles, and 20% on everything else. We've also added a new Friends of AK ebook program: $15 a month gets you an electronic copy of every book we publish for the duration of your membership. Combine it with a print subscription, too!

There's great stuff in the works—so sign up now to become a Friend of AK Press, and let the presses roll!

Won't you be our friend? Email friendsofak@akpress.org for more info, or visit the Friends of AK Press website: www.akpress.org/programs/friendsofak